RISE UP

RISE UP

AND TRULY LIVE...

ROB STEARNS

Consumed Publishing

Consumed Publishing
An extension of Consumed Ministries.
Bloomington MN, 55420
www.consumedministries.com

Consumed Ministries is a message centered ministry that exists to
share the message of abundant, overflowing, more than you can
begin to imagine life found only in knowing God in a deep, inti-
mate and relational way.

Edited by Stephanie Frusher
Cover art by Ilona Bergmann
Design and layout by Tammie Davis & Eric Beavers

Published in Minneapolis, MN by Consumed Publishing.
Printed by Bethany Press International
6820 W. 115th Street
Bloomington MN, 55348

Unless otherwise noted, Scripture quotations are from the HOLY
BIBLE: NEW INTERNATIONAL VERSION. Copyright ©
1973, 1978, 1984 by International Bible Society. Used by permission of Zondervan Publishing House. All rights reserved.

ISBN 978-097665551-0

Library of Congress Control Number:

Printed in the United States of America.

TABLE OF CONTENTS

Dedicated to my wonderful children, Meaghan and Nathan.
My prayer is that you'll never stop dreaming, that your love for
Jesus will continue to grow, and when you grow up, that your
dreams will set this world on fire!

I love you both, with every fiber I have.

Special Thanks:
To my parents—for always believing in me and encouraging me
to follow my dreams. I love you both.
To my kids—for being exactly who you are. And for keeping the
dreamer in me alive. I love you.
To Volker Loh—vielen, vielen dank für deine Hilfe. Du bist ein
Vorbild für mich. Danke.
To Ilona Bergmann—das du da bist, auch wenn ich bin so unsich-
er. Und für ein wünderschönes Cover. Danke.
To Jamie Miller—this is entirely your fault. You have been an
example to me in the way you have "recklessly" followed the
Holy Spirit's leading in your life. If more men were like you,
the world would truly be "consumed." You came "out of the
blue" and encouraged me to write. None of this—my writing
or dreaming—would have happened without you. I am so
grateful for your role in my life.
To Eric Beavers--for doing all the work behind the scenes and for
answering all my questions...every time...every day...every
week...and being so patient. Thank you...I will never bug you
again (well, at least not until tomorrow).

And most importantly, *The Holy Spirit*—I am just now beginning
to feel the magnitude of your presence in my life and just how
powerful you are. Forgive me for ignoring you for so long. You
have guided me through stretches of my life the past few years
that I couldn't bear alone, but you held my hand the whole
time—even when I wasn't aware. You have remained faithful
to me, just as you promised. It is because of you, Holy Spirit,
that I am unashamed to approach my Father.

INTRODUTION

The birth of this book came from the combination of many things. First, and foremost, it came from the pain in my own life. Pain from Satan and further pain from my trying to take matters into my own hands. Secondly, this book was born when I was simply encouraged by a friend to write. Another factor contributing to this book was the Scripture I was introduced to during sleepless, tear-filled nights.

But the thing that made this book come alive, was not a thing. It's a who. The Holy Spirit. He has guided me and shown me things in the past two years that could only have come from above.

And now, although my life is far from perfect or even remotely smooth, I am beginning to see things from a spiritual perspective. I am beginning to see what my life could be if I let God lead. I am beginning to see what my life could be like if I step up and treat Satan and sin for what they are—mine to rule over.

But there is so much more. I'm seeing what life could be like for this world if we, as Christians, would take the reigns of our lives and rise up to become the children of God that we are called to be.

My prayer is that this book would be an encouragement to Christians around the world and be part of the process that the Holy Spirit is leading them on—or, at least trying to lead them on (our stubbornness can be a huge distraction).

I honestly yearn for Christians to rise up out of the sleep that has become our lives and wake up to realize how wonderful and incredible our lives could be if we would follow the dreams that God has given us. I yearn for us to be all that God created and for us to take this world over for His Kingdom.

I.
THE PRE-BEGINNING

Have you ever watched a movie, oh, let's say 253 times? You know every scene, every character, every voice inflection, and every costume by heart. Then something small in the background catches your eye ... a book on a bookshelf, a particular song in the soundtrack, the symbolism of the name of a character, a particular building or street corner, or a quick line-in-passing from a bit-part actor. All of a sudden, the meaning of that scene takes on larger significance. In that moment, the movie's main character has additional dimensions. Suddenly, the meaning of the movie has changed. Not only has the meaning changed—but it has profoundly affected you personally. You spend the next few days mulling over that small, little something and then you think to yourself, "Aaahhh, now I get it."

Something like this recently happened to me. But it wasn't just one little thing, it was several major things that came crashing into my life at the same time and I wasn't prepared for what was about to happen to me. It just happened.

I was reading the Bible. I was honestly seeking answers in God's Word. To most Christians, running to the Bible would be an obvious choice. But that wasn't all. The Bible wasn't the only "source" infiltrating my life. I was daydreaming. I mean, really daydreaming— I was imagining myself in a cause that was bigger than me, I was imagining what life would be like if I could just accomplish a specific dream. During this time, I saw a movie at the local grocery store and decided to get it—*The Devil's Advocate*. And to top it all off, I was dwelling—

and when I say "dwelling," I mean the sleepless uneasy meditation—on my uncertain future and becoming increasingly scared.

And then it happened. It happened—that small little something took on a greater significance. The meaning of my life raged up inside of me like a speeding rapid waiting to rush over its banks. Suddenly, the plot line of my life changed. The protagonist took on a bit part. And the bit-part actor took over the lead.

Oh, to be alive—truly alive. And to feel it. To know it! Carpe Diem!

Now that my stream-of-consciousness writing has probably confused you, I guess it makes sense to start at the beginning.

Or, to be more precise, the pre-beginning. Not my beginning. Our beginning.

God is in heaven. Three in one. The Father, the Son, and the Holy Spirit are all ruling the heavens in a vast expanse. Angels are in abundance. Legions. Thousands. Tens of thousands. Angels are armored with the most heavenly of all armor, and are waiting to fight with and for their God and King. Angels ready to serve, no matter the command.

Lucifer, the most beautiful angel of them all, rebels against God. Living in perfection and with perfection was simply not good enough. Lucifer had to have more—not unlike us sometimes, eh? Pride. Original sin. Greed. Desire to be the one in control, to have the power to call the shots, and to be like God. He wants to be just like God. This is only mentioned twice in the Bible, so it's pretty important that we understand what it says. We pick up the story, the pre-beginning, in Isaiah 14. Let's look at verses 11 to 15:

> *Your pride has been sent down to the places of the dead. The music from your harps goes with it. Flies are spread out like your bed beneath you, and worms cover your body like a blanket. King of Babylon (Lucifer), morning star, you have fallen from heaven, even though you were as bright as the rising sun! In the past all the nations on earth bowed down before you, but now you have been cut down. You told yourself, "I will go up to heaven. I will put my throne above God's stars. I will sit on the*

mountain of the gods, on the slopes of the sacred mountain. I will go up above the tops of the clouds. I will be like God Most High." But you were brought down to the grave, to the deep places where the dead are.

Satan has fallen. He's gone—banished from heaven. There is nowhere to go. If this were a movie, we'd be watching Satan and his army of demons trying to gather themselves back together, dusting themselves off from the angelic war they had just lost. The screen fades to black, while Keith Richards' introductory guitar riff to Paint it Black is playing as background music. Satan turns to look back at the camera, one eyebrow raises, and the corners of his lips curl. He has a plan, and its objective is vengeance. He'll show up again in the upcoming act.

The scene then changes to God's beautiful creation: The virgin world. Untouched. Inhabited by two creatures, just like you and me … created directly in His image. Take a moment to reflect on this scene.

A sky untouched by high-rises, smog, or phone lines. At night the stars shine brilliantly with no city lights to drown them out . Snow-capped mountains rise up in the distance, and green valleys are free of villages, roads, and shantytowns. Trees, newly created, are stronger than buildings of steel. The grass so plush you can almost bounce off it—not unlike it is in Ireland. Water so clear and clean you can see the fishes' brilliant colors and the beauty of the coral reef all the way at the bottom. Streams so pure you can drink out of them. Birds are singing, uninterrupted by the sound of traffic. A fire is crackling. Two people, Adam and Eve, not unlike you and me, gaze around at beauty perfected. Looking into each other's eyes just like a young couple who walks into their newly purchased home, as if to say, "Can you believe this is ours?!" While they are taking this in, they are actually taking a walk through their neighbor-hood with God. Talking to God. Totally unashamed to be in His presence.

I've got to be honest. I'm not looking

forward to this coming Friday. You see, at our church we take communion every Friday night. I'm not exactly sinless, and I can't possibly imagine what it is like to be in God's presence without being embarrassed by my sins, my decisions, and myself. What is it like to be so pure that one can just go for a walk with God and not be ashamed by His holiness?

And yet, Adam and Eve were taking walks with God! Adam and Eve—who were humans like you and me. The sun sets on perfection. Adam and Eve fall asleep in each other's arms. The angels nod in agreement, as they stand guard. The Godhead smiles. Adam and Eve begin to fall into a deep, fulfilled sleep.

The screen fades to black once more.

Bongo drums echo and a man is screaming like a monkey shrieks in the jungle. The sun rises on the garden and the distinct voice of Mic Jagger begins to sing:

"Please allow me to introduce myself, I'm a man of wealth and taste. I've been around a long, long year, stole many a man's soul and faith…Pleased to meet you, I hope you guess my name, but what's puzzling you is the nature of my game." The Rolling Stones, Sympathy for the Devil

Satan re-appears on the scene. He and his demons have nowhere to run, he's no longer welcome in heaven and roaming in the vast expanses doesn't seem to thrill him. So he hides. He waits. Then he decides to reside in God's own backyard, in perfection itself. He thinks, "If I can keep these humans from reigning over me someday, that's good. But if I can find a way to banish God's precious little souls to Hell, all the better. They can have paradise – for now – but it will be mine soon, and to Hell with their souls!"

We know the rest of the story. We're living it out.

Suddenly, and yet so quietly, Satan polluted perfection. And we, the human race, never saw it coming. Sadly, we still don't see him coming today. Far too often, Satan is still a surprise. Shame on us.

II.
WHY ARE WE HERE?

Why are we here? What is man's purpose? Why did God put me on this earth, with this genetic make-up, to be raised in the States, to live in Germany, to have two beautiful children, and to end up where I am now? Why? To what end is my life?

I don't think I'm alone in asking these questions. Throughout recorded history, man has been asking the same questions. King Solomon, the wisest of all humans, sought the meaning to life and recorded his thoughts in Ecclesiastes. "To be or not to be," wrote

31

Shakespeare. I can go down to the local library or look at my own bookshelf pick up *The Purpose Driven Life* and read away ... and thoughts about a life of meaning begin to dance through my head. Why am I here?

I'm not going to offer you any answers to those questions. Most of the time, I can't seem to figure out my own life. How in the world am I going to offer somebody else any help? But I do think I know Someone Who just might have the answers.

What is my purpose? Why am I here? I think God gives us some pretty definite answers to those questions ... often maybe we just don't take the answers seriously. Or maybe, and this is much worse, maybe we don't even know the answers God has given us to these questions. And here's the tricky part—I don't think these answers always come from the Bible. They come from the Holy Spirit, they come from our hearts, and they come from places we're just not prepared to accept.

And by the way, it is exactly at this point in my life—the search for these answers—that I found those little subtleties that changed the scenery of the movie that is my life. Better yet, these little subtleties have changed the landscape of the outlook of my life!

Before we get to matters of the Holy Spirit or our hearts as being the source to our purpose, we should probably at least know what God has created us for. I think it's safe to say that God did not just make us to take up space. We are very safe in assuming that He had something more important and regal in mind for us.

God put Adam and Eve in the middle of the Garden of Eden for what purpose? To enjoy it? Most definitely. But was that the only reason? In Genesis 2, we read that God put them there to care for the garden. To tend God's garden. To tend the earth. We are to take care of this planet. Now, one might say, "Ok, but that was then, and only until they got kicked out of the garden. And this passage speaks specifically of the garden in a perfect world and not of the earth." Well, I beg to differ.

I believe that this earth is ours, and I'm not alone. God does too. It is our job to take care of this earth. Think about what we, as Christians who are heirs to this world, could do if we started campaigning for this planet. Think about it! Global warming, the rain forest, the hole in the ozone, pollution, and reusable fuels would be important. Economic greed and mass consumption wouldn't be what drives us. Making as much money as possible—just because we can—would take a back seat to making sure God's creation remained as well kept as possible. Now my mom might get angry with me for sounding like a "tree hugger," but if God gave us this planet, I think we should take that responsibility seriously.

I'm not just talking about planet responsibility. I'm also talking about exploring this planet and having fun with it—climbing its mountains, running through its forests, skiing on its waters, and rafting down its rivers. I'm talking about owning it!

When we own something, don't we normally take good care of it? I hate giving out my DVDs to friends because one time someone broke my copy of Monty Python's *Search for the Holy Grail* (I think you know who you are). For that reason, I am protective of my things. I don't want what is mine to be returned broken. And that's a stupid DVD! What about things that matter? What about our earth?

The last thing I want to do is to start an environmental campaign, so let's move on. What other jobs have we been given by God?

What about judging? I'm not talking about accusing everyone and his grandmother of doing wrong. I'm not suggesting that we piously point out every single sin that those around us commit. There may be a time and a place for that, but according to Scripture, before we can do that we better be sure that we are above reproach and that the sins we are pointing out are removed from our own lives. I'm talking about judging in the sense of justice—making sure things in our world are fair. I'm talking about being a voice for the voiceless and champions for justice.

Leviticus tells us to judge in righteousness. Proverbs tells us to judge righteously, and Proverbs tells us to take up the causes of the poor and needy. Isaiah tells us to seek judgment, relieve the oppressed, and provide help to widows.

Part of our reason for existing is to make this world a better place—through judgment, or, better yet, through justice. It gets better, as far as judging is concerned.

Paul tells us in the sixth chapter of 1 Corinthians that we are going to be judging angels someday. What is that all about? We are going to be placed higher than angels. Is it just me, or is our role in God's plan getting a bit more significant?

Now, let's take this a step further. What are demons? Angels, right? Fallen angels, that is. Well, if we are going to have the opportunity to judge these terrible spirits someday, what about judging them now? Right now!

I'll touch on this later—but keep this very important thought in mind.

We've been talking about judging, but what about ruling? Revelation 22 paints a vivid picture of the New Jerusalem. God's servants are there, and they are worshipping God. Let's pick up the scene …

There is a beautiful new city, built on a hill. Nothing guilty will be found in this city because it is God's Holy City. We are its inhabitants, but we are not alone. Saints, who are beautiful like angels, are there from centuries past. No decrepit bodies, no limps, no wheelchairs, no leprous flesh, and no disease are in sight. Angels surround the city, and their armor glitters with the light of God Himself.

We, who are God's servants are there, and:

"They will see his face, and his name will be written on their foreheads. There will never be night again. They will not need the light of a lamp or the light of the sun, because the Lord God will give them light. And they will rule as kings forever and ever."

Wow! We are going to be ruling as kings. We are going to be rulers.

Let this soak in: we were created to make this world a better place. We were made to take care of this planet. We were created to rule, and we were created to reign.

Once upon a time, humans were pure. We were holy. We now have sin in our world and in our lives. But God still pleads with us to be holy. He pled with the nation of Israel, and Peter reiterates this plea in his first epistle. God says, and I'm paraphrasing here: "Be holy because I am holy." God is pleading with us *to be like Him.* This is not intended to make our lives difficult; it exists because He is perfection. He wants us to experience that—even with our sin— right here on this very earth.

You don't quite follow me? Let me explain. God is pleading with us to try our hardest to be holy. I admit living a holy life is pretty difficult. I mean, just five minutes ago I sinned. I let bitterness get a hold of me. And just yesterday, I took a peek at some Internet sites I shouldn't have been looking at. Oh yeah, and I got mad at my kids the other day and reacted in a way that wasn't pleasing to God. You get the idea.

Is it even possible to be holy? Seriously, why does God command us to be holy when there is no way we can? Why? Because he wants something better for us. He wants us to be better off than what we are! Isn't that how all proud parents think? Don't we want our children to be the best they possibly can?

In 1 John 2, we read something that is so exciting it could only come from God Himself! We read that we, who are His children, *know God*. We read that we have *defeated sin* and that we have *defeated Satan*. We read that our sins have been *forgiven!*

Through Jesus' death and resurrection, we are no longer sinners. We are holy. Right now, we are holy. We are not slaves to sin. Satan is no longer our father. We are holy!

Through Christ's blood we are able to regain that image of God that we were originally created with.

III.
WHAT WE WERE
NOT MADE FOR

There's always another side to the story. There's always the flip side. There are two sides to every coin. And so it is with us.

If we were created to be perfect, if we were created to be holy, if we were created to be God's, then it should go without saying that we were **not** created for imperfection, that we were **not** created to be full of sin, that we were **not** created to be someone else's. We were **not** created to live a life of defeat.

Let's go back to the Garden of Eden to the point where Satan makes his entrance. *Sympathy for the Devil* is playing in the background, and a snake, a slithering creature who was wisest among the animals, saunters up to Eve. Does he force Eve, and her husband, who is standing idly by, to eat of the forbidden tree? Does he show her through logic that it is okay to take its fruit? No.

He deceives. He lies. He steals pure innocence. Satan, in this moment, steals man's immortality. And, quite literally, he steals man's soul. Our chance for perfect communion with God is now destroyed, because Satan stole us from our Creator.

God will now spend centuries trying to regain our lost love. It is up to us to respond. God calls out to us through His creations, through relationships, through great men and women, through song, through newborn babies, through visions, through His servants, and through His Word. God calls out to us in specific yet varied ways. It is up to us to listen and respond. It's up to us to seek and to knock.

The fact remains: Satan stole us. We did not originally belong to him.

I remember as a very young child watching a group of men coming off an airplane on TV. My mom was ironing. She stopped and stood there weeping. I couldn't understand what was happening. My mom was crying because those men were American troops coming home from Vietnam. They were tears of joy. Why? Because those boys were finally coming home. My mom and dad lost friends and fellow-soldiers in Nam. Those young men who sacrificed their lives were not going to be coming home. But now a whole planeload of those boys—now men—walked across the screen. My mom simply became overwhelmed by her emotions and wept tears of joy for them because they had survived.

Ask yourselves why the Bible says the angels rejoice when someone accepts Christ as his Lord and Savior. Why? Because that soul is coming home! That soul has been rescued … and heaven is full of rejoicing. Those angels know that a soul has survived a vicious battle. That soul has been rescued and will someday be coming home, to where he or she belongs. We were made for God. We were not made to be Satan's possessions. The fact that he had to lie to us and deceive us to get us away from God proves his thievery. We were not made to be sinners. We were not made to be ruled by sin. When God made us, we were perfection. We knew no sin. Revelation paints a futuristic picture of the New Jerusalem where nothing "God judges to be guilty" will be there. Perfection will exist once more. Sin is a result of Satan. It was his pride, which led to his banishment from heaven, which ultimately led to his deceptive attack on mankind. Sin was not part of what God wanted for His children.

Don't get me wrong. I don't want to introduce the "devil made me do it" card for all the bad things in our lives, or the decisions that we voluntarily make. We are responsible for our decisions. When tempted by sin, by desire, by lust, by anything, it is our choice to follow it or to resist it. We have a free will. Our free will allows us to follow God or follow Satan. The ball is in our court, so to speak.

And that is where the beauty lies. The ball is in our court. Because God made us to be pure, that part of us is still alive in us ... somewhere. Somewhere, deep down, in the depths of our souls, the desire to be perfect and pure still burns. Oh, this desire might be smoldering just a bit, but it is there. God made us perfect, and His ultimate goal is for us to be perfect (2 Corinthians 7:1, Ephesians 4:12).

And the thing is, we know it. We want to be perfect. And if we can't be perfect, we want to be as good as we can, do we not? If you don't believe me, ask yourself how many times you look at yourself in the mirror to make sure your hair or make-up still look good. If you belong to a gym or lift weights at home, how often do you flex your muscles in the mirror to see how "ripped" you are or to check out how flat your stomach is getting? How many self-help books are sold and read every year? Face it. We all want to be better than we are.

I'll admit we are far from perfect right now. I guess I can't speak for anyone else, but I can assure you that I am the furthest thing from perfect—on the outside and the inside. But is it possible to try and change that? Can we take on another mindset that will help us become all that God created us for? I think the answer is: most definitely! We were not made to be defeated. In his first letter to the Corinthians, Paul asks the questions: "Oh death, where is thy sting? Oh grave, where is thy victory?" (KJV). Sure, our bodies will grow old and weary and will someday die, but our souls were not meant to be defeated, especially by death. And to prove that, just two verses later, Paul says: "But thanks be to God, which giveth us the victory through our Lord Jesus Christ." (KJV) Translation: we've already won!

In Revelation 15, John records a vision of those who "had gotten the victory over the beast" (KJV). Translation: we've already defeated Satan!

Romans 6 tells us: "Sin shall not have dominion over you..." We were not made to be defeated by sin. We were not made to be ruled by sin. Sin is ours to rule.

I am positive that sin is ours to rule. I will cover this later. But for now, if you haven't been able to come to grasp with this concept, let it ruminate in your thoughts. Let the fact that we were not made to be ruled by sin settle in. Let the fact that we can rule over sin take root.

IV.
GOD'S KINGDOM

What does it mean to be a future ruler with Christ? What does it mean to be a future judge of angels? What does it mean to have defeated sin? What does it mean to be holy? Well, I think it depends on your perspective. Or, more specifically, one's perspective on the Kingdom of God.

Is God's Kingdom taking place right now? Or will it be established at some point in the future? Hmmm. You know what? I'm not going to jump into that argument right now. My (lack of) intelligence is prohibiting me from taking this argument on. But I will say this. I have been struggling with this for the past few years. Ever since I read *Paradise Restored* by David Chilton.

His argument is that the Kingdom of God—although it may not look like it to the untrained eye—is happening right now. And that we, as Christians, better wake up and start taking our roles in this Kingdom very seriously and quickly. I won't rehash his book right here, although I highly recommend your reading it for yourself. Reading *Paradise Restored* sent me on a quest, if you will, and here are some things that I have found in regards to whether or not God has established His Kingdom right now. If we start out with the word kingdom, we'll find a bunch of passages that seem to deal with God's Kingdom in the future … I don't think there is any doubt here. Jesus Himself spoke of a futuristic Kingdom. However, Christ also told those around Him that the Kingdom was upon them (Luke 11). He told us to seek the Kingdom. He also taught that one of the signs of the Kingdom would be the destruction of the Temple and that the "gospel of the Kingdom" would be preached throughout the world.

The Temple was destroyed in 70 A.D. and the "gospel of the Kingdom" has been, or is being, taken across the world as you read the words I just typed.

Acts gives us a great account of how Paul and Peter went around the known world preaching the Kingdom of God and things "concerning the Kingdom of God." Hebrews tells us that Jesus is at the right hand of the throne of God, and that this throne is forever and ever. John records in Revelation that he saw a vision of God ruling along with the Lamb that was slain.

If the Bible tells us that Jesus is ruling at God's right hand, wouldn't it make sense that He is ruling at this very moment? In the present tense? Thus making Him a ruler? Thus having a kingdom?

If God's kingdom is truly forever and ever, then does it really make sense that He would be taking a break? If Satan is truly the ruler right now, wouldn't that make him more powerful than God? And didn't we already see that Satan has already been defeated?

I'll be honest. Some of this goes against my Baptist upbringing. I was always taught that a rapture would happen and then there would be three and a half years of peaceful, good times on earth followed by three and half years full of horrible events, orchestrated by the Anti-Christ before God comes back to claim heaven and earth for His own thousand-year reign. My pastors and professors had proof texts and everything. With this outlook on God's Kingdom, my job was to endure and to try and be holy, even though I was a rotten sinner, while waiting for death or the Rapture. Not a very joyful or exciting outlook.

I'm struggling with this even now. But I'm starting to believe that God's Kingdom is for now. I'm starting to look at this life in a completely different light. I'm thinking that God hasn't called us for the future. He's called us for now!

And, I'll be honest. God calling us for the "now" scares the life out of me. It really does. It's one thing to think of being a ruler, a king, or a judge serving in some future kingdom. Think back to all the history classes you had or all the books you read about knights, kings, castles, and kingdoms. All those stories had war as the central theme. And wouldn't it make sense that if God has established His Kingdom, that it would come under attack from Satan, or, worse yet, is under attack right now?

In *The Devil's Advocate*, Al Pacino's character, John Milton, is the Devil disguised as a lawyer. The closing scene in the movie very accurately depicts just how tight a grip Satan seems to have on this world by explaining his role on this earth:

I'm here on the ground with my nose in it since the whole thing began! I've nurtured every sensation man has been inspired to have! I cared about what he wanted and I never judged him! Why? Because I never rejected him, in spite of all his imperfections! [Furiously] I'm a fan of man! I'm a humanist. Maybe the last humanist. Who in their right mind, Kevin, could possibly deny the 20th century was entirely mine? [Yells] All of it, Kevin! All of it. Mine. I'm peaking, Kevin. It's my time now. It's our time.

Go look at the front section of your daily newspaper, turn on CNN, or listen to the news on the radio. If you don't have time, I'll give you a recap:

Africa is dying away through draught, starvation, and AIDS. The Middle East is in an uproar over cartoons, and they are blowing each other up over sectarian beliefs. Israel and Palestine are fighting (again). Bird flu is spreading quietly, yet quickly. Child porn rings are being busted; others are not. Murderers are escaping from prison. Men convicted of war crimes are dying or committing suicide in prison.

Tsunamis, hurricanes, earthquakes, and landslides are killing people by the thousands.

I'll admit this doesn't look like much of a great kingdom. If this world were supposed to be God's Kingdom, you'd think He could do a better job, right?

But don't forget the question: If God has established a Kingdom, wouldn't it make sense that it would be under attack from Satan? What about our jobs? Didn't God give this world to us? Isn't it our job to take care of it? If God's Kingdom is for now (and if it is, it sure is in shambles) shouldn't we be *defending* it?

And here's the worst thing about it all: It's our fault for not seeing it coming. Or worse yet, for ignoring it once the attack came. Just as Eve choose to look the other way, so do we.

Then again, he is the deceiver. How did Satan tempt Eve? With deceit. How does Satan tempt you? I'll tell you how Satan tempts me:

through sweet-nothings. Whispering in my ear, consoling me, stroking my ego, easing my pain, telling me that my "vanity is justified" (Satan, *The Devil's Advocate*).

Whether or not God's Kingdom is for now, or for later, or for both, I think it is safe to assume that Christians are under attack from Satan on a regular, frighteningly real basis. And this attack from Satan seems to justify the reality of God's Kingdom. If God were not reigning, why would Satan be so active in his attacks against God—especially today.

Satan appears to be more active now than at any other point in history, besides when Christ was on Earth.

In a three-minute long song, *Sympathy for the Devil*, Mic Jagger tells the historical story of Satan's role in the world in the past 2000 years. The Rolling Stones give an accurate account. Starting out with Pilate washing his hands, Satan moves forward to the Russian Revolution, makes a cameo in World War II and plays a role in decades of man's wars. Satan is alive and kicking. We are under attack right now, and sadly, we don't even know it.

Again, I want to refer back to Pacino's role as the Devil. He has a great monologue towards the beginning of the movie. He's talking to Kevin, his protégé, and ends up describing how he, Satan, works:

Don't get too cocky my boy, no matter how good you are. Don't ever let 'em see you coming. That's the gaffe, my friend. You gotta keep yourself small, innocuous. Be the little guy. You know, the nerd, the leper ... Look at me. Underestimated from day one. You'd never think I was a master of the universe, now, would you? ... You're missing what I have ... I'm a surprise, Kevin. They don't see me coming. That's what you're missing.

Just as the Bible tells us, Satan is on the prowl. He is looking to attack us, ever so quietly. He wants to make sure that our souls remain stolen. He wants us. But he's not going to appear on the scene—or at least the scene we are able to see—screaming your name, waving a sword, or drawing attention to himself. Oh no, he's much wiser than that. As Paul wrote, Satan is hunting us like a lion...crouching, hiding, picking up our scent of fear, eyeing our soft spots, while focusing on our jugular the whole time.

So, what does this all mean? What is this talk about jobs or roles that we may have? What about this attack by Satan? Is it so real? What's all of this about?

It means that God wants a Kingdom established, if it is not established already. It means that Satan is attacking this kingdom, and it means that we are under attack. It means it's time. It's time to rise up!

V.
WHAT DOES THIS MEAN?

I've been asking this question for a few pages now. What does all of this mean? To be honest, I don't think it's hard to find the answers to all of this. The hard part is putting it into action. What does it mean to be God's creation or God's possession? It means that we belong to the one, true God. It means that He wanted us, so He made us—in His image, no less. Then through Satan's deceit, He lost us, so He fought for us and is continuing to fight for us. And ultimately, He wants something more for us!

What does it mean to be a part of God's Kingdom? It means that we are going to be rulers with Him someday—maybe even today. What does it mean to have defeated Satan and sin? It means that we have a say in whether or not sin controls us. Instead, we control sin. What does it mean to be dead to sin? It means that we are alive!

One of my favorite passages in the Bible is from the last verse of Isaiah 40. I know it is an oft-quoted verse. But oft quoted verses are usually worth quoting – even quite often. I was first introduced to this passage by U2's rendition of this passage in their song, Drowning Man:

> *Rise up, rise up*
> *with wings like eagles*
> *you run*
> *you run*
> *you run, and*
> *not grow weary.*

It is time for us to rise up. We are under attack! It's time for us to rise up and spread our wings!

In *The Twin Towers*, the second install-
ment in the *Lord of the Rings* trilogy, we are introduced to King Théoden of Rohan, who has
spent some serious time under an evil spell cast
by the malicious wizard, Saruman. Through the
help of the wizard Gandalf, Théoden is released
from this spell. Once he is released, he learns
that his son died trying to defend the people of
Rohan, from evil orcs who are roaming his lands
and killing everyone in their way and that a highly organized orc army is on their way to attack
his city. Gandalf and Aragorn are there to help
offer guidance. The king is concerned for his
people and fears an impending war against one
of two dark forces, the armies of Sauron and the
armies of Saruman, if not both of them.

Two Rohanian children, who have
escaped the razing of their town and been sent
away by their mother towards safety, come to the
castle of Rohan and are taken in by the Princess.
They are scared, have just reported the attack
and the destruction by the orc army, and are eat-
ing their first good meal in days. This is where
Gandalf and Aragorn try to step in:

Gandalf: This is but a taste of the terror that Saruman will unleash. All the more potent for he is driven now by fear of Sauron. Ride out and meet him head on. Draw him away from your women and children. You must fight.

Aragorn: You have 2000 good men riding north as we speak. Éomer is loyal to you. His men will return and fight for the king.

King Théoden: They will be 300 leagues from here by now. (Pause) Éomer cannot help us. I know what it is you want of me, but I will not bring further death to my people. I will not risk open war.

Aragorn: Open war is upon you, whether you would risk it or not.

Open war is upon us whether we would risk it or not. We can choose to run away and hide, or we can ride out and face the battle we are in. We are under attack, whether we choose to accept it or not. It is now time to rise up and take on our roles in this war!

How we view our lives is how we are going to live our lives. It's that simple. Our perception of our lives will determine how we are going to define our roles in this battle.

Before I explain my point of view here, it is important to realize what I am not saying. I am not coming across as some sort of motivational speaker passing on a pep-rally diatribe, "Buck up there partner! You can be all that you can be, you just have to believe in yourself!" I am not talking about visualizing your dreams and then coming up with a 12-step plan to accomplish those dreams. I'm not talking about putting little encouraging notes around your home to remind you of what you can become.

I am simply saying that if we view ourselves as being downtrodden and defeated, then we will live that way. Whereas, if we live our lives like there is still something worth living for, a fight still worth fighting, and a God worth sacrificing for, then we will live as something more than what we are. At least, we should.

If we view our lives as something to endure until the end, just struggling with sin until death or the rapture then that is how we are going to live ... as struggling, fatalistic people waiting for death.

If we view ourselves as slaves to sin, or at least slaves to a particular sin, we will allow ourselves to be ruled by it. It becomes a self-fulfilling prophecy. Sin will rule over us. How do I know this? Because this is how I lived in the past. I let bitterness rule me because I felt sorry for myself. I allowed lust to rule me because I felt I couldn't stand against it. You know the saying: if you can't beat 'em, join 'em. I have been there. I struggle with this mindset even as I type this. The battle is not over.

If we view ourselves as pathetic sinners, who are not forgiven by Christ or who are unworthy of forgiveness because our sin is too great to be forgiven, then we will ultimately accept sin in our lives because sin belongs to the sinner. We will allow sin to fester in us like a disease.

In the climatic scene of *The Devil's Advocate*, the Devil, in a heated argument with his protégé, Kevin, gives a great illustration of what I'm trying to explain here. Kevin is trying to defend his actions through some sort of "entrapment" argument claiming he was set up by the Devil. The Devil responds by pointing out that all the bad deeds Kevin performed were actually his, Kevin's, decisions, thus throwing the guilt back into Kevin's lap. But at the end, the Devil turns to Kevin, and says, "Your vanity is justified." In other words, the Devil's arguments range from, "You are disgusting. You are the one who is filthy, and who could possibly want to forgive those sins" to "But it's okay. You're not so bad, your sin is justified … it will all be fine."

The Great Deceiver, indeed.

But there is once again—the flipside. If we view ourselves as fellow servants with Christ, doesn't it make sense that we'll begin to act like a servant of Christ? If we start to view ourselves as rulers, wouldn't it make sense to start ruling over things in our lives that need to be ruled over?   Things like lust, laziness, worry, or _____.   Again, I'll touch on this later.

If we start to view ourselves as kings of an eternal Kingdom, wouldn't we start to act like it?   Wouldn't we start to see our lives here on earth in spiritual terms as opposed to physical?

Being a basketball fan and growing up near Chicago, I have no choice but to own a DVD about the Chicago Bulls championship teams of the 1990's. After the Bulls won their first championship, the team underwent an attitude change.   That change was best seen in Scottie Pippen. He had a "forget you all" attitude and despite having Michael Jordan on his team, he set out to dominate his opponents. Teammate John Paxon, who according to my mom is the most gorgeous of all the Bulls, said that Pippen had a certain arrogance about his game after that first championship. Pippen simply said: "Once you become a champion, you gotta walk, carry yourself like a champion." As a result the Bulls went on to win five more championships in the 90s. They acted like champions. They continued to win championships. They were champions.

Scottie Pippen knew he was a champion. He acted like a champion. He lived like a champion. Then he played like a champion. Don't we know we are children of God? Are we acting like it? Are we living like it?

It's time for us to rise up! It's time to spread our wings and show the world that we Christians are no longer slaves to the dark forces of this world. That we have been given keys to an eternal Kingdom from our Eternal Father. It's time to start inviting others into this Kingdom.

VI.
AND YOUR POINT IS?

I'm finally getting to one of my main points. I'm finally getting to the small aspects of the story that I discovered that give me a whole different perspective of the movie. I want to share with you what I've found. The discovery that is making me burst at the seams.

But first...I need to share with you what I am not saying.

It may seem odd, but I need to do it for my conscience's sake. I am saying that it is time for us to rise up and start ruling as kings. I am saying that it is time for us to take over the sin in our lives.

I am not saying that being a king is going to be easy. I am certainly not saying that once you decide to follow Christ everything will be great. I am definitely not preaching some sort of "health and wealth" gospel—follow Christ and you'll remain healthy and wealthy.

No. Just the opposite.

Once we decide to follow Christ, Satan is going to be hot on our trail. Christ told His followers that the world would hate them. He told His disciples that they would be killed because of their preaching of the Kingdom. Once we follow Christ and take His blood seriously, our lives will never be the same!

Oh to be alive! To be ALIVE!

What does John 10:10 tell us? The first part of the verse tells us that Satan is hunting us. And to what end? To kill and destroy us. He hates us so much that not only does he want to kill us, but he wants to destroy everything in our lives.

Satan hates me so much that he destroyed my family. He lured me away from my Christian responsibilities as a husband and then lured my wife away. And the worst part? I get to see my kids once every fourteen days, and I hate it. When I have to drop my children off after I get to see them every-other weekend, my son runs back to me weeping. I hold him, grab his hair, and hug him. And inside my ex-wife's new apartment that she shares with her new lover, I weep. I cry and hold my son like no other father has ever held his son, and I weep. I tell him I love him, but there's not one thing I can do about his torn heart. Then I get to drive home for an hour and cry.

Why is that the case? Because Satan hates me and wants to destroy everything in my life. I could stop right there, let the pain overwhelm me, and start to feel sorry for myself. I could let Satan win. I could give up.

But I can't. I can't give up. That's only half the story.

The verse goes on. "But I have come to give you abundant life." Jesus closes out the verse with a proclamation of victory. In other words, Jesus is saying: Although Satan will try to kill and destroy you; I will give you life so abundant that it swallows up that death.

Oh, to be alive! And maybe, just maybe, the only way to know you're alive is to feel pain. If you aren't feeling pain, maybe you are dead.

The past couple of years have been tough for me. They have been years of immense spiritual growth and major spiritual disappointment. As soon as I would start getting closer to

God, I would find deception just around the corner waiting to drag me closer to hell.

On one hand, I was reading and getting excited about being active in an eternal Kingdom. I was psyched to think God could somehow use me—that He would *want* to use me. On the other hand, I was letting bitterness towards my ex-wife eat me alive. This bitterness was robbing me of sleep, but I was the one allowing it.

I was reading passages in the Bible and having my eyes opened to a very real spiritual battle, that was taking place in my world and yet I was running to the arms of a woman who wasn't my wife. I was the one running. I was the one reading the Bible by day and running away by night.

I was being challenged by the writings of C.S. Lewis and John Eldredge. I was writing myself. I was reading different Psalms every day. And yet, I wasn't letting anything sink into my heart completely. I wasn't allowing the Word of God and the encouragements from other Christians to become lights to my feet and lamps to my paths.

I was full of head knowledge, yet I became a fool of head knowledge.

But through this struggle, I realized a few things. I realized that I was alive. I realized that the pain in my heart was real. And if my heart had no feelings, then it was dead. As much as I hated the pain of sin in my life and as much as I hated the weight of a guilty conscience, I knew that having it meant that I wasn't dead yet. I still had a pulse!

I realized that Satan was attacking me for a reason. He's attacking you for a reason. Think about this for a moment. Why would Satan attack me? You? Christians in general?

Why? Seriously. Why doesn't Satan just leave us alone? Why doesn't he just give up on us and start attacking souls he can actually take to hell?

Because we are dangerous. We are alive. We are the key to his demise. We own him!

One tactic to coaching basketball is to attack the best player on the team when you are on offense. The reason? Hopefully that player will get tired or better yet will pick up a few fouls and will have to sit on the bench. If you're really lucky, that player will get too many fouls and will have to stay on the bench. And even if the player hasn't fouled out, he can't be as aggressive as he wants because he can't afford to be out of the game if he picks up another foul. So you attack that player, make him work hard, tire him out, and force him to the bench. Once he's on the bench, and out of the game, the team is weaker.

If Satan can take you out, then the team is weaker. He's attacking you because you represent something to him that he fears. You are dangerous in his eyes, that's why he is hunting you. He is attacking you because he fears you. We Christians are the best players on God's team—if we're not being attacked, maybe we're not one of the more valuable players.

Satan fears us. Satan is scared of Christians.

Let me explain.

VII.
CARPE DIEM I

Okay, I know that I've babbled on long enough. I've talked about a variety of ideas and never really let on about my "discovery." I haven't shared what little nuances to my life's "movie" I actually found. I'm getting to that; I promise.

I have read every book of the New Testament at least once with the exception of 1 and 2 Corinthians. I'm not sure why. I just never read through them or studied them. Finally, I figured it was a good time to start. Ironically, I ended up reading 1 Corinthians 7 on the day of my divorce. As I type this, I suppose I should be honest about the fact that I'm still not done reading through them. Apparently, I'm a slow learner.

I read through 1 Corinthians 3 about twenty times for a college project. Maybe that's why I never read the rest of the book. Anyway, I started reading through 1 Corinthians and nothing really fazed or struck me. A couple verses stood out and were worth underlining, but nothing made me just gasp. Until I got to the last three verses of Chapter 3:

All things belong to you...the world, life, death, the present, and the future—all things belong to you. And you belong to Christ and Christ belongs to God.

Wait a minute.

All things belong to me? *All things?* All things! My talents belong to me. My dreams belong to me, and what God has given me belongs to me.

RISE UP

The world belongs to me. I cannot wait for next summer's cycling trip to Italy or Norway. Those fjords and Alps belong to me. God has given me the earth as a gift. Now I know why that green grass was so soft in Ireland when I got thrown off my bike last summer. That green grass was my gift.

My life belongs to me. Satan can't have it. Satan has no say in what I do with my life. It's mine, not his. Satan has a say in my life only if I let him. But that's my choice.

My death. O glorious death, where is your victory? Where is your sting? It's gone. My death belongs to me. This means that I can embrace death because it's actually my entrance, my pathway, my beginning to a new, eternal life. Death no longer reigns over me. Yes, my body will die, but my soul? Never!

But this keeps getting better. I'm just touching the tip of the iceberg here. The present belongs to me. Right now belongs to me. Carpe

Diem! Seize the Day! God has given me today, the immediate present. This is my day!

And it goes on. The future is mine! The dreams I have for the future, the things I want to accomplish, they all belong to me. Satan can't have them. The future is mine. I don't have to let Satan control my future!

Now, before you think I'm getting cocky or selfish, let's look at the closing verse of this passage once more: "You belong to Christ, and Christ belongs to God."

The future is mine, and the present is mine. My life and my death are mine, along with this world. Yet, it is all in the context of belonging to Christ. We can simply look at Christianity throughout the Bible and see that when people started living for themselves, their lives became empty and were not by blessed by God.

But what about those people who obeyed God? What happened to them? A couple of things. First of all, they were opposed in every possible direction. They were hunted by Satan himself. They were not allowed to simply just do great things for God. Why? Because they were entering a spiritual war and going toe-to-toe with the Devil himself. Secondly, those people seized the day. They rose up and did incredible things that history still recounts! Even better, they did things that will be recounted for all eternity. They experienced great pain, yet they lived!

Right now, I find myself starting to realize the immense freedom there is in Christ. Just think about this: the world, the present, the future all belong to me. They belong to you! They are ours and it is up to us to do with them what we please. We can either do things to please ourselves, or we can do things to please God, things that will echo in eternity.

I don't want to paint a picture of me being some sort of super-Christian, some sort of warrior who knows no fear. Coming face-to-face with Satan scares me, as it should. Did Paul instruct us to put on the Armor of God and fight? No! He told us to pray—to run to God.

Let's face the facts here. As romantic as it may be to think that I can stand above Satan with my foot on his heaving chest as he slowly breathes his last breaths, with me, the hero, standing above him with a stained sword waiting for God to approve my delivering the final blow, that is not going to happen. Satan will devour me. He is the great deceiver, and he knows my weaknesses and how to exploit them. Satan has a centuries-long résumé of tempting people and destroying lives. I have no choice but to run to God.

The beauty is this: through God's victory and Jesus Christ's blood, we have dominion over Satan. We have won the battle.

This is where that second little "discovery" comes into the movie.

I was at church on a recent Sunday when my mind started drifting away from the sermon. Now before you start to criticize me for drifting off, I know you do it too. Besides, I have to listen to the sermons in German and sometimes I get lost. So, what I'm trying to say is that I have a better excuse than you! Anyway...

I ended up in Genesis reading the account of Cain and Abel., and I found something I had never seen in that passage before. I had always just read over it without it having an impact on me. After Cain and Abel bring their sacrifices to God we see that God only accepts Abel's. This upsets Cain. I guess since this decision is the catalyst for Cain committing murder, it might be safe to say he was a little more than upset. Yet, before Cain kills Abel, God actually has a little conversation with him. And it goes like this:

The Lord asked Cain, "Why are you angry? Why do you look so unhappy? If you do things well, I will accept you, but if you do not do them well, sin is ready to attack you. Sin wants you, but you *must rule over it.*" (emphasis mine)

Sin wants us. Satan wants us, and we know why. He wants to destroy us and to destroy everything around us because we are his enemy. The bad news for him is that we are victors over him, which makes him desire all the more to take us down.

Sin wants us, yet God replies: "But you must rule over it." Therefore, <u>it must be possible for us to rule over sin</u>; God would not command us to do something that is impossible. We can rule over sin. We are able to rule over it, because God made us that way—able to defeat sin. And just to make sure, He took it a step further. He sent Christ here to defeat death and sin and the Devil for good!

And now my "movie" has a new meaning. The antagonist, the Devil, has a revised, diminished role. The hero (that's me!) has a greater role—a much more dangerous role—one that has him rising out of the ashes of his life to become a warrior in a battle most of us can't see. The future dreams and plans of this hero will now play a major part as the plot of this movie thickens.

We can rule over sin! We can rule over the Devil! We can take the pain that Satan tries to throw in our lives and have dominion over it. Remember when we talked about judging angels someday? I tried to make the point that demons are fallen angels. Since they are technically angels, we will be judging them, and we will be in control. What about judging their actions in our lives right now? What about judging them as guilty and then casting them away in the name of Jesus Christ? What about taking domain over the parts of our lives which demons seem to control?

I'm serious! I'm not talking about coming up with some sort of exorcism where you become like Linda Blair, sleeping in a floating bed with a rotating head. I'm talking about taking control of our God-given lives and judging Satan and his coworkers and letting them know that they no longer have permission to rule over you!

This may sound a bit extreme to some of you; it even looks awkward as I type it. But I don't think I'm too far off of what God wants for our lives. Does He want us ruled by demons? Does He want us to allow ourselves to be ruled? NO! He pleads with us to rule over sin and to take control of it before it takes us down.

We can take the doubts that Satan whispers in our ears and rule over them! We can take the sin in our lives and rule over it sometimes by running away and sometimes by calling on Jesus to help cast out demons. We can take our fears and rule over them. We can rule over anything Satan can throw at us.

Don't take my word for it. Take God's!

VIII.
THE NEXT STEP?

Where do we go from here? Even Axl Rose once sang: "Where do we go? Where do we go now? Where do we go?" That's a great question—very legitimate.

I'm not going to try and answer that question for you. Or for Axl, for that matter. I have no idea who you are, how God is challenging you, what attack Satan is throwing at you, or what visions God is giving you. I can only speak for myself.

This is what I want to see happening. For now, I want to focus on my general vision.

I want to start taking the sin in my life seriously. I want to rule over it and throw it out of my life. And you know what? I am. Because God has given me that ability, I'm going to rule over it.

I'm going to start praying much more fervently. Without serious help from God and his angels, I cannot continually keep Satan in check in my life. I know Satan will be knocking on my door soon. I know he's going to try to keep this book from ever seeing the light of day. I know he's going to continue to seek me out, so he can destroy me. I need back up. And I figure going to the One who has already defeated him is a pretty good plan.

I also want to do something great—something unbelievable! You know what I want to see? I want to see a worldwide reformation, and I want to be a part of it! I want to see college campuses full of students burning with a desire to know more about God. I want to see the Middle East experience mass conversions of Muslims choosing to follow Christ. I want to see people in Western Society rejecting humanism and evolution and embracing God once again. I want to see Christianity spreading through the world of sports, through the world of academia, through the world of music, through the world of performance art, through our individual worlds!

I want to see people not giving in to sin. I want to see Satan confused about where to go! I want to see him scared of returning to Heaven and confused as to why he is no longer wanted on this planet. I want to see a world that is praising God and going all out to serve Him. I want to see generations of Christians taking this spiritual battle so seriously that they are on their knees in prayer ruling over the sins that once used to rule over them.

I want to be on the front lines of this battle, and I want my visions to become a reality! I want to be able to present my dreams and visions to God someday as living sacrifices. I want to see my dreams put on God's altar, and I want to see His holy fire devour all the debris in my life, and then I want to fall on my knees and humbly see that those dreams and visions weren't just pipe-dreams and that what I did with my life mattered and didn't burn away. And I want to hear Him say, "Well done."

I definitely have dreams and visions of what I want to do to for God. I'm sure some, if not most, of you do too. What about writing that song that's been lingering in your mind for some time? What about calling up those friends who want to form that band and take the message of the Kingdom to the masses through lyrics and music? What about starting that company or ministry you thought about a long time ago? Remember when you discovered how good you were at working with a certain group of people? The elderly, junior high students (God, please grant me patience with those kids!), grade school students, autistic or mentally challenged, the physically disabled, or the emotionally disturbed. Remember when you used to feel something for a specific group of people?

Who do you think gave you those desires? Who do you think led you to discover those gifts? Who do you think put those visions or dreams in your mind? Satan? Whatever. Since when is Satan a compassionate being? Are you the source of those visions? You? Please! God is. God has given you those things; God has shown you those things, and they belong to you!

Your visions, your desires, and your talents—they all belong to you. "All things belong to you … and you belong to Christ, and Christ belongs to God."

And you know what? God gave those to you for a reason! He wants you to rise up, He wants you to take those visions and run with them. Use them to preach, or sing, or draw, or perform, or scream, or whisper, or simply touch someone to show them the Kingdom of God.

You will be attacked. Oh, you'll be attacked. Jesus even said so. But isn't that a good sign? Doesn't that just prove that Satan is angry and that he wants you out of the picture? Doesn't Satan's attack verify how much God loves you and how valuable you are to Him? And doesn't Satan's attack prove just how dangerous you are to him?

Isn't it time? Isn't it time to rise up and rule over sin? I can't possibly imagine living the rest of my life as a defeated soul under Satan's rule. We must rule over sin. It's time to begin ruling. It's time to begin reigning with our eternal King!

It's time to rise up and spread our wings. It's time to dream ... and dream big!

IX.
WHAT DO YOU DREAM ABOUT?

"When you dream, what do you dream about?"

...pens the lead singer of The Bare Naked Ladies, a band from Canada, which should explain their name, as he watched his newborn baby sleeping soundly.

I wrote this poem for my children about a year ago:

Sleep Tonight
for my kids

Sleep tonight
Sleep, sleep, sleep
Eyes so heavy
Dreams so near
Sleep my darlings
Dream your dreams
Then awake
Your dreams to chase

Why are parents so concerned with the dreams of their children? Is it because we lost our dreams at some point? Is it because we want to see our kids live life in the wonder of a fairy tale world? Is it because we ache deep inside from not pursuing our dreams? Is it a combination of things? To be honest, I'm not sure.

The rest of this book is about dreams. It's about visions. No, to be more accurate, I guess it's more about vision. I'm not talking about having a vision like John had when he wrote Revelation or the kinds of dreams the Old Testament prophets had when God told them exactly what to say or do.

This book is about the desires that are in our hearts. It's about those childlike dreams we have for our future. The kind of dreams that we had when we wanted to be an astronaut one day and an NFL quarterback the next. The kind of dreams that have my daughter, at the age of eight, trying to figure out if she wants to be a ballerina, a teacher, a missionary, or a painter. The kinds of dreams that have my son wanting to be Spider Man (which, when you think of it isn't so bad ... you get to fight crime and kiss Kirsten Dunst) and a pirate.

Let's shift the question away from our children and onto us. What did you dream about as a kid? What are you dreaming about now?

When I talk about dreams and visions in this book it's not about being talked to by God directly. But I am talking about being talked to by God indirectly. I'm talking about God talking to us through our hearts, our desires, and other people.

When we start listening to His whispers and start letting ourselves get moved by His slight nudges, then our dreams begin to take place. At least, I hope they do. They have for me.

I'm 35 now, and I'm just now starting to figure out that dreaming is okay! Why did it take me so long to figure this out? How did I allow my dreams to be stolen? Why don't we recognize our new dreams as they change through the course of our lives? What happens that causes us to lose the desire to follow our dreams as we get older? Who stole my dreams and my ability to dream? I hope to answer some, if not all, of those questions in the remainder of this book.

I'd like to start out with us, or, actually, with me. Maybe I'm the only dreamer out there, but I have to ask whether you are happy with where you are in life? Do you dream of doing more with your life? I'm not talking about having more: a bigger paycheck, a bigger car, a bigger house, a better job, etc. I'm talking about doing more. Are you happy with where you are? If so, I commend you. Personally, I'm aching inside. At the same time, I'm like a volcano waiting to explode. I need to let myself out. I need to let my dream out and pursue my life!

Let's start by looking at the world of poetry. Don't worry, I'm not talking about poets from the Romantic Period or some obscure French poet who wrote about wood bridges in some daisy-filled prairie. I'm talking about today's poets, musicians, or, more accurately, lyricists. Isn't it amazing how sometimes a song just nails your thoughts exactly and leaves you wondering why you'd never thought of that line before? And if you've never wondered that, then you've never been in love. I find that the world of music, especially, "secular" music often gives

us great insight into man's deepest longings of
the soul.

One of my all-time favorite songs of is
Dream On by Aerosmith. I think anyone who has
grown older or is in the process of some sort of
self-introspection can relate to this song.

> *Every time that I look in the mirror*
> *All these lines on my face getting clearer*
> *The past is gone*
> *It went by like dusk to dawn*
> *Isn't that the way*
> *Everybody's got their dues in life to pay*
>
> *I know what nobody knows*
> *Where it comes and where it goes*
> *I know it's everybody's sin*
> *You got to lose to know how to win*
>
> *Half my life is in books' written pages*
> *Live and learn from fools and from sages*
> *You know it's true*
> *All the things come back to you*

Sing with me, sing for the year
Sing for the laughter, sing for the tears
Sing with me, if it's just for today
Maybe tomorrow the good Lord
Will take you away

Dream on, dream on, dream on
Dream until your dreams come true

Don't we fit this song perfectly? Life has passed us by from "dusk to dawn," we've got dues in our lives to pay just to get by, it seems like we're not getting anywhere and everything in our life will come back to us—albeit hauntingly. If only we could just sing. If only we could just let our souls out.

This has never been more apparent to me than in the past year. I turned 34 last year, and my dad called me up to wish me happy birthday. There's nothing odd about that; it's a rather normal thing for a parent to do. But then he told me that I may as well enjoy this year because next year, I'd be half-dead. Ouch. My dad is a really funny guy, but some truth still exists in that statement. Statistically, my life is about half over. Do I have anything to show for it?

Back to the lyrics of *Dream On*. What does Steven Tyler sing for the chorus? Here is a man who doesn't know Christ and yet he sings "Sing with me just for today, maybe tomorrow the good Lord may take you away." This man sees the finality of not living a life worth living.

This could almost be compared to *Two Step*, which is by the Dave Mathews Band: "Eat, drink, and be merry, for tomorrow we die." And where do these guys get the inspiration for songs like this? From the Bible! But they're missing something. They're missing the point of having a life of purpose!

When Paul wrote, "Let us eat and drink, because tomorrow we will die," in his first letter to the church in Corinth, he was talking about living a life not worth living. Paul was saying that if his life was not worth living, if it was a life not worth sacrificing for God, then he, and the other Christians, may as well just live for today. But a life lived for God, a life lived with a purpose, is a life worth living to the fullest. It's a life worth grasping!

Both of these men are coming from the perspective of "you only live once ...," and they are both right. Even the Bible tells us that we will all die. But they are taking that phrase and adding to it, "... so you may as well have as much fun as possible." But Paul takes the attitude that you only live once so we may as well give everything else to God, to a cause higher and greater than we are. Paul says in 1 Corinthians that "if the dead are not raised" we may as well eat, drink, and be merry. Wow! Raising the dead! Talk about taking a cause with him to the grave and into eternity.

Do you want to be living out a life that doesn't have a calling, doesn't have a greater purpose? Do you want to just live for today?

Personally, I fear that. I fear living for today. I don't want to lay my head down on my pillow and realize that I accomplished nothing of eternal value..

X.
DREAMERS - I

Take a moment to think about great men and women of history who had dreams. Great men and women whose dreams not only led them to glory, but whose dreams actually changed the world.

Martin Luther was a Catholic priest who began to see the injustice that the Catholic Church was handing down to its own congregations. And through his struggles of being a conscientious priest, he began to have two dreams.

The first of which was to reform the Catholic Church. Most people think that Luther set out to break away from the Catholic Church, which he did since he was excommunicated, but his original goal was to *reform* it. He never wanted to be out of the Catholic Church; he wanted to *improve* it.

And all of his dreams of reform started from his reading through the book of Romans. While reading Romans, he was impressed upon by the Holy Spirit about two major things. The first was that we are "saved through grace" rather than by a religious institution. The other thing that was planted in Luther's heart was the importance of having the Bible readily available in the language of the people. In other words, instead of having the Bible read in Latin during church services, why not make it available to the masses in their language, which in his case meant German.

As a result, the Bible began to be translated into the languages of the people; it was translated into French, German, English, Danish, Swedish, etc. For the first time in history, people were able to read the Bible in their own languages and, thanks to the printing press, in their own homes.

What happened next became known as the Reformation. How far and wide is the influence of the Reformation? Just answer these questions: How many Bibles are in print today? In how many languages? Why do the Slavic nations have crosses on their flags?

God moved mountains because of one man's dream.

George Washington, by all accounts, was a great man. You have to be if you can handle false, wooden teeth. I love the Revolutionary War Era of the United States because the patriotism was pure. Freedom and dying to preserve it were honest and highly regarded. Being a patriot meant something. It meant being part of something that transcended the mere individual.

I don't think we see this patriotism any clearer than in the movie *The Patriot*. Gabriel Martin, a young soldier fighting in the Revolutionary War, writes a letter home to his brother Thomas, who reads the letter to his younger sisters:

> *I envy you, your youth and distance from this cruel conflict of which I am a part. But I consider myself fortunate to be serving the cause of liberty. And though I fear death, each day in prayer I reaffirm my willingness, if necessary, to give my life in its service. Pray for me. But above all, pray for the cause.*

Sure, that's Hollywood for you. But the men and women of colonial America had everything to lose for their freedom—their land, their possessions, their money, their lives, and their children's lives were all at stake. Everything they had, they stood to lose. Everything.

One of my favorite stories about George Washington is one that displays his humility rather than discussing his teeth. It's not about his crossing of the Delaware River. It's not about his rallying his troops while they were dealing with frostbite. It has to do with a humble spirit.

George Washington wanted a free land. He envisioned something bigger than colonies. He envisioned something more than just George Washington the Great War Hero or George Washington the "American King George." He feared that the position of leader of this newly freed country would be feared by some and revered by others. It was a position that would be coveted and easily be abused, but he was willing to put his life and the lives of his men on the line for it.

After being elected leader of this newly freed country, when asked what he should be called, George Washington simply said, "Mr. President." No "King," no "highly exalted ruler," no "Mr. Ruler," and no B.M.O.C. (Big Man on Capitol Hill). Washington's dream was of a free country where power would not be abused. What was the best way he could prevent abuse even from himself? By humbling himself and making his title one that gave deference to the citizens of the new country. Washington exemplifies a dreamer with a conscience.

Susan B. Anthony was a female suffragist whose ideas and values resonate all the way from the Equal Rights for Women movement to today's government to the movie Mary Poppins (I have a daughter; I need to know these things). Now, I'm not a big fan of the Feminist Movement, nor do I pretend to be. But take a look at what life is like for women in the Western world compared to our sisters in other areas of the world.

How many rights does an average Middle Eastern woman have compared to a Western woman? How many baby girls were killed due to China's One Child Policy? How many women in Africa have had their bodies mutilated in the name of tradition? How many women have been murdered by their own families in the name of honor because they had been raped. Why aren't the rapists killed?

In those societies, women and their rights and their dreams are not valued. It was women, like Susan B. Anthony, who pushed for equal rights, not allowing their dream to die or their voices to be silenced even though they were "only women."

Einstein is considered by many people to be one of the most intelligent people who has ever lived. His equation, $e=mc2$, is probably the most recognized scientific equation, and the bane of my high school science experience. Did you know that Einstein wasn't exactly your typical valedictorian? The man, who shaped modern science more than any other individual, was considered a slow learner, who may have had dyslexia or even autism (Wikipedia). At one point, he was a high school drop out. That's amazing. Do you think his life was easy?

This kid didn't have it easy. What do you think he dreamt about? What was his motivation? Why didn't he just pack it up and quit or get a job working for his father's business? Why did he have to identify this important equation and ruin my grade point average? Why?

Because he was a dreamer! And you know where he got the inspiration for his theories about time and space? From watching the workings of a mechanical clock and staring at his reflection in a mirror. The guy is sitting around, watching a clock and checking his hair. He's just the most brilliant daydreamer ever.

No talk about dreamers can be complete without mentioning Martin Luther King, Jr. I'm going to let his words speak for themselves. I've underlined the words that have left an impact on me:

Five score years ago, a great American, in whose symbolic shadow we stand signed the Emancipation Proclamation. This momentous decree came as a great beacon light of hope to millions of Negro slaves ... One hundred years later, the life of the Negro is still sadly crippled by the manacles of segregation and the chains of discrimination ... still languishing in the corners of American society and finds himself an exile in his own land ...

It would be fatal for the nation to overlook the urgency of the moment and to underestimate the determination of the Negro ...

We must forever conduct our struggle on the high lane of dignity and discipline. We must not allow our creative protest to degenerate into physical violence. Again and again we must rise to the majestic heights of meeting physical force with soul force ...

We cannot walk alone. And as we walk, we must make the pledge that we shall march ahead. We cannot turn back ...

I have a dream that one day this nation will rise up and live out the true meaning of its creed: "We hold these truths to be self-evident: that all men are created equal." I have a dream that one day on the red hills of Georgia the sons of former slaves and the sons of former slave owners will be able to sit down together at a table of brotherhood. I have a dream that one day even the state of Mississippi, a desert state, sweltering with the heat of injustice and oppression, will be transformed into an oasis of freedom and justice. I have a dream that my four children will one day live in a nation where they will not be judged by the color of their skin but by the content of their character. I have a dream today.

RISE UP

Few little girls are inclined to study science or math. I'm not going by statistics here—I'm just saying, few do. And then Sally Ride enters the scene and takes on the worlds of science and math and the male-dominated world of astronauts becoming the first woman in space. I have to admit; I'm not the biggest supporter of the space program, yet two things about it still inspire me. The first is the opportunity it provides for us to see earth from the space shuttle. What a view! I'm always in awe when I see those photos.

And the other is when you see someone like Sally Ride go against the odds and persevere. She's not just plugging away for her own gratification. At least, I hope not. Women like her are now role models for my little girl, which means a lot to me. My little girl can look at women like Sally Ride and dream of seeing the world in a way only few have. What were Mrs. Ride's dreams as a child? Does my daughter have some of the same dreams as she did? What's my little girl dreaming about right now?

What about the contributions of Bob Geldof, former lead singer of The Boomtown Rats, and Bono, lead singer of U2? It's not a secret that I'm a huge U2 fan and that I love music from the 1980s. Even if you don't share my sentiments, you can't argue that Bono and Mr. Geldof aren't trying to do something good in the world.

Geldof organized 1985's Band-Aid fundraiser to end hunger in Africa and has campaigned tirelessly since then. Bono has formed his own ONE Campaign to end, among other things, debt in Africa. These two "rockers" have been trying to get the Western political powers like President Bush, Prime Minister Blair, and Pope Benedict to help end starvation in Africa, reduce or abolish Africa's debt, and end sectarian violence in Northern Ireland and Africa.

These men have more money than the average person can even imagine, yet they want to make a difference. Rocking a stage is one thing, having 80,000 people sing the words to

Psalm 40 with you is another. Trying to help an entire continent and actually doing something about it is completely out there. Once again, we have dreamers. Dreamers with great vocal cords, but dreamers who get something done.

XI.
DREAMERS - II

Now let's start to bring this back to the point. The point is that we live lives of purpose, lives of meaning. But not just lives of meaning that we feel good about. We can all argue that our lives have meaning. I'm talking about meaning for God. Meaning that lasts for *eternity*.

Let's look at the life of Nehemiah. His story is a great example of having a life with meaning, with a purpose larger than himself. Yet, this purpose has to do with living a life for God and doing something great for Him. Once we see what he was dealing with, I think we can start to wake up in our own lives. Not only wake up, but also start dreaming.

Nehemiah was an Israelite, a slave. He was also a servant of the king. He was the kind of well-liked servant who enjoyed nice living arrangements and being well fed. I'm sure he had nice clothes too. King Artaxerxes probably didn't want any slobs in his presence. Nehemiah even had a decent job: he served the king his wine. Not exactly a bad job if you can get it.

So here's a slave whose life isn't half bad. He probably lived at the castle or in the surrounding suburbs. For a slave, he had a pretty good life. He wasn't outside in the heat or rain planting and harvesting crops, building fortresses, or hauling building materials through the desert. Life, for all practical purposes, was good for Nehemiah.

Then he gets some bad news. Fortunately, this bad news spurs on his dream.

He finds out that back home in Jerusalem his very own people are the laughing stock of the region. His hometown has lost its protective walls, leaving it with no defense against invading armies or nomadic thieves. Jerusalem, the Holy City of God, was becoming nothing but a barren wasteland compared to what it used to be.

Nehemiah weeps. His heart is broken. He mourns for days, praying to God the whole time. This is his prayer:

> *Lord, God of Heaven, you are the great God who is to be respected. You are loyal, and you keep your agreement with those who love you and obey your commands. Look and listen carefully. Hear the prayer that I, your servant, am praying to you day and night for your servants, the Israelites. I confess the sins we Israelites have done against you. My father's family and I have sinned against you. We have been wicked toward you and have not obeyed the commands, rules, and laws you gave your servant Moses. Remember what you taught your servant Moses, saying, 'If you are unfaithful I will scatter you among the nations. But if you return to me and obey my commands, I will gather your people*

from the far ends of the earth. And will bring them from captivity to where I have chosen to be worshiped. They are your servants and your people, whom you have saved with your great strength and power. Lord, listen carefully to the prayer of your servant and the prayers of your servants who love to honor you. Give me, your servant, success today, allow this king to show kindness to me.

Nehemiah is in pain. His heart has been broken. This is not just about himself; it's about his people, his God, and his hometown. Not only is he in pain, he's in no position to do anything about it. He's miles from home, and he's a slave who has no freedom to act. How in the world is an expatriate slave going to do anything worthwhile?

But Nehemiah was more than just an expatriate slave. He was a dreamer. Let's look at his dream on two levels. The first is the earthly level. We all have dreams at the earthly level, don't we? Whether it be hitting the game-winning basket, getting the girl, having Mr. Right fall for you, rising up through the ranks of your particular business, turning your community into a better place for kids, saving whales, or reducing auto emissions, we all have dreams that we want to see come true. We catch ourselves daydreaming about what life would be like if our dreams came true.

Nehemiah was no different; he had a dream, a really big dream. He wanted to see his city's walls rebuilt, he wanted to see his countrymen living in freedom, and he wanted to see the Israelites back in the Holy City, Jerusalem.

Just keep in mind how difficult it would be to make this dream come true. He would have to convince Israel's captors to free all the Israelites so they could go back home. In other words, Nehemiah had to get these rulers to give up all their free labor. He was going to have to gather all the Israelites up and bring them back home—this was going to be a huge, logistical, travel nightmare, and it had to be done without the benefit of Orbitz, Travelocity, or a travel agency. And at some point, they were going to have to rebuild the city's stone walls by hand.

Nehemiah wasn't just dreaming. He was dreaming big -no **huge**- dreams. One could even argue that he was dreaming an "impossible dream."

That thinking is earthly thinking. Nehemiah takes it a step further—a lot further. Nehemiah takes his dream straight to God. And not only does he take his dream to God, he challenges God with it.

Go back and look at that passage again. Nehemiah pleads with God to look and listen to His servant. Then he calls God out on God's promise to Moses. Basically he is saying: "God, I remember what your promises are. I've read what you told Moses. We have to repent, and we have to live our lives for you. Just as you promised to punish us, you also promised to reward us and take care of us if we are following after you. God, please listen to me!"

God is a God of Truth. He is Truth. He can't go against His own Word, which Nehemiah knows. I would go so far as to say that God loves it when Nehemiah calls Him out on it. Why would God love this? Because one of His own children has remembered His teachings. One of His own children is bold enough to dream big. One of His own children is pleading for His help. How does Nehemiah end this prayer? By saying, "God, give me success."

Before we get excited and start running to God to plead for success, we need to keep this at the forefront of our minds: Nehemiah knew that any success or blessings from God would be based upon his obedience. Before we can approach God about our dreams we must be obedient to God first.

Nehemiah had the gall to ask God to listen to him, not once but twice. He also had the gall to ask God for success. How does God respond? He gives Nehemiah the things he requested, which is proof that God loves it when we come to Him with our dreams. He looks at His little dreamer and decides to help.

Nehemiah wasn't just a clueless dreamer, though. He was a calculating, thoughtful dreamer; he knew exactly what he wanted. He had a vision of exactly how he was going to accomplish his dreams. He had thought through how many workers, how much time, and how many supplies he needed. He had even considered how he would present the idea to the king.

Nehemiah was still under mental duress about his dream; he couldn't even sleep at night. I'm not sure if you've ever been there or not, but I haven't been able to sleep for the past three weeks. I have a dream and I can't get a decent night's sleep. I feel like Nehemiah.

Nehemiah still had to talk to the king about his dream. But once he had the opportunity, he didn't hold back. Not only did he ask the king for time off, he asked the king for travel documents that assured safe travel, which meant free passage, plus a police escort, and for building permits. To top it off, Nehemiah had the gall to ask for building materials. Again, he was dreaming big. The king's response was: "Okay, sounds great. Have fun. Send me a post card."

Nehemiah dreamt big. Keep in mind the fact that his dream coincided with God's will.

XII.
DREAMERS - III

The people we've looked at so far did great things because they had dreams and vision. Let's take it a step further. Actually, let's take it a step closer—a step, or two, closer to us and to our hearts. What about the visions that we have in our own hearts and souls that are screaming to be released?

I'm going to tell you about my dream. I've already shared it on a general level, but now

I'm going to get a bit more specific. While I'm sharing about my dreams, I want you to think of your dreams. I want you to let your dream expand while allowing God to mold it.

To be perfectly honest, my dream consists of two parts. I realize it's a bit greedy, but I want to dream big. If I can't dream big with the one, true, all-powerful God in my corner, then when is dreaming worth it? So I'm going to dream big.

The first part of the dream is to write. I want the world to hear what I have to say. I want people to grow closer to Jesus Christ through what I write, and I want my writing to challenge a generation of Christians much like Martin Luther's Ninety-Five Thesis did or John Eldredge's many books do today.

You see, I've been dreaming of writing for about a year now. The seeds of that dream were planted long ago. I can remember the first short story I wrote. It was called The Van and was based on an orange Match-Box® conversion van I had. Don't ask. It was raining outside, and I was bored. I have, however, been writing poetry since college. The problem is that I had been keeping my desire to write a secret.

I had been keeping my poetry a secret in order to maintain any type of masculine street-cred that I may or may not have had. I had been writing poems no one would ever read. I always thought about writing, but all I had to show for it was a half-hearted attempt at a book about basketball for boys, poems stuffed in manila folders inside a box in an attic and a children's story, *The Lonely Blue Sock*, for my daughter. There have been no essays in *The New Yorker*, no Pulitzer Prizes, nothing.

It seemed that the only place where my thoughts were being read were in emails I was writing to my friends. Yes, if it hasn't been confirmed by now, I am a dork. Through these emails, I had a medium to write and work on my humor and my style and actually form a coherent thought or two. Then one day in March 2005, I received this email:

> *Rob,*
> *Have you ever thought about writing?*
> *Jamie*

That email became the catalyst that woke up a dreamer. That email was confirmation. I'll write more about the idea of confirmation later.

One could argue that that particular email created a monster. I've been thinking about writing constantly since then. I've written poems—and actually let people read them. I've written some essays, and now I'm writing this book. I'm a writer possessed. I love it!

Like I said, I want these writings to be read by the masses. I want people who read this to rush to read their Bibles and to pray asking God for forgiveness and direction in their lives. I want to be on the front lines of a literary Reformation movement.

That may seem arrogant and more than a bit conceited. But why should I not have big dreams? Do you want to hit the game-winning shot or do you want to be on the bench when it happens? A friend of mine was once asked what he would do if money were no object. He said he'd go to Africa and start clean-plumbing projects for shantytowns; that sure beats installing a new toilet in your house while remodeling, does it not? Let's dream big dreams.

Yes, I'll say it—*I want my books to reach the masses!*

Discussing that part of my dream leads to the second part of my dream. I want to cycle around the world. I want to have a cycle-tour company that takes young men on bike tours through Germany, the French Alps, Ireland's coasts, the Rocky Mountains, up and down California wine country, and wherever a road or bike trail leads.

I want to take these guys on these tours and make their lives miserable. If you've ever been on a bike seat for six or more hours a day, then you know what I mean. As we're being knocked off our bikes by high winds, getting sun-burned by the noon-sun, struggling up mountain passes, and speeding down hills, or, um, mountains, at speeds that I can't print here because my mom will get mad at me, I want to sit down with these young men at the end of the day, relax, enjoy a hearty meal, maybe smoke a pipe, plan our route for the next day, and talk to these guys. I mean *really* talk to them: find out where they are in their lives, what they want to do, what they dream about. Most of all, I want to share Christ with them.

I want to take these guys on a great vacation, where we'll be experiencing nature pure, fighting against the elements (the sun, rain, wind, mountains), fighting together to get to Point B, and all the while share with them Jesus Christ and His love for them. I want to make a difference in young men's lives—one tour at a time, one summer at a time.

Those are my dreams—to write and to cycle. I realize that writing poems and wearing spandex shorts aren't exactly adding to my manly persona, but I think they can be considered the necessary evils that accompany my dream.

And just think of all the possibilities these dreams open up. Writing about new subjects, doing research on new ideas, meeting new people from cycling, seeing different parts of the world, and possibly visiting hospitals in other countries after being thrown out of my saddle could all happen as I pursue my dreams. Seriously, think of the people I could meet. The more people I meet, the more people I can help impact.

These dreams are why I'm bursting at the seams to get outside of myself and start living!

XIII.
THE SOURCE OF OUR DREAMS

I hope I don't sound ultra-spiritual here, but I am going to go on record as saying that I believe our dreams come from God. Think about it logically for a moment.

Most of your dreams about what you want to do with your life come from your desires or your talents, right? I have a good buddy here in Germany who was working for a travel agent. He was good at his job and loved the travel business, but he didn't like his job. He and another co-worker, Gunther, who I didn't really need to mention except that I thought it would be cool to type the name Gunther, were making over 70 percent of the travel agency's business. They both had the dream of running their own travel agency. One day they got to talking, and now they are co-owners with their own travel agency, Terramundi, which, I'm happy to add, is doing very well.

How many teachers have dreamt of a better way to teach a subject because they were bored stiff with the curriculum and their love for their students drove them to a better teaching method? How many people have decided to break away from their jobs and at least try to make it on their own?

Now if these dreams come from our talents or our desires, ask yourself this: Who gave you those desires? Who equipped you with those talents?

God. Period.

Now the Devil, and even we, can manipulate these talents and desires, but I'm asking about the source of our talents and desires. God gave them to us, and they come to us because He gave them to us and He allows for it.

I've wanted to cycle since I saw Lon Haldeman win the Race Across America (RAAM) as a young boy. My infatuation grew when I watched Greg LeMond win the Tour de France on the last day of the race. Then Lance Armstrong battled cancer, doubters, and the rest of the field to win Tour de France seven times in a row setting a record. Since the seventh or eighth grade, I've wanted to be a cyclist. God has put that desire in me, and He has kept it there.

What dreams do you have? How long have you had them? How long have you been brushing them aside or sleeping on them? And just whom do you think gave them to you?

Look, if God gave you those dreams, don't you think there's a reason behind it? Don't you think maybe, just *maybe*, He wants you to go for it? Better yet, don't you think He's *longing* for you to get out there and take the world by storm?

When we're truly focused on God and our dream takes the world by storm, in effect, God is taking the world by storm, and He receives the glory.

Doesn't it seem like dreamers do all the great things in this world? Why is that? Because they had a crazy idea and followed through with it. If our dreams come from God, doesn't it make sense He's going to give you strength to see it through?

This does beg a question, though. How do we know if our dreams and visions are coming from God? I think it's safe to say that if our dream or vision is strictly for our benefit, then it's not from God, or it's a dream that has been hijacked by the Enemy. If our dream is for our gratification, I don't think we can take much comfort in the hope that God is behind us.

But there's still another way we see if our dreams are from God—confirmation. Let's go back to Nehemiah. Getting a free pass from the kind, permission to build Jerusalem's walls, and the supplies for the project were not exactly requests you just go and approach the king about, but God confirmed Nehemiah's dream in several different ways. The first one was that Nehemiah couldn't sleep. I'm not suggesting that indigestion, insomnia, or any other reason we can't sleep is always confirmation that God wants us to do something. In Nehemiah's situation, God would not let him forget about Jerusalem. God kept Jerusalem in Nehemiah's heart and mind. This dream possessed him.

The fact that the king granted all of Nehemiah's requests was another sign. I can imagine Nehemiah getting ready to go to Jerusalem still somewhat dumbfounded by everything:

Okay, do I have everything I need. Clean socks ... um, yeah. Clean underwear ... got it. Sword, sandals, favorite travel shirt (because every man has a favorite travel shirt ... we just do). Now, the important things.
Time off from being a slave: check.
Police Escort: yep
Building Permits: right here
Blank Check to buy materials: got it
Okay, God, what are we waiting for? **Let's go!**

From a human perspective, these requests were impossible. You can almost see Nehemiah down at the local pub drinking a Coke and telling his buddies that he's going to the king tomorrow to ask for time off, a paid vacation, and the money for the building materials to go help repair Jerusalem's walls. Can you imagine their reaction: blank stares, wide-open mouths, then hysterical laughter.

But we know what happened. God provided! Today we say things like: "Well, God will either open or close the doors," which is true. But if God is opening the doors to our dreams, we better run like the wind through those doors. What are we waiting for?

By providing for him from the beginning, God confirmed that He was the one providing Nehemiah's dream. In Nehemiah 2, he says that God was kind to him—not once but twice. He's making a point of letting us know that God was taking care of him and that God wanted this to happen.

Now let's look at the flip side. What if God didn't want Nehemiah to do this? Do you think Nehemiah's dream would have been met with open doors? I doubt it. This is where we need to really look at our lives and see when God is opening up doors for our dreams and when He is closing them. Is God closing them permanently? Maybe. Is He putting it off for timing purposes? Could be. But we have to face the fact that there are times when what we want is just not happening.

I've been trying for years to find a way to teach here in Germany. I've tried everything; there isn't an avenue I haven't tried except lying or extortion, though they have crossed my mind. Nothing. Nada. Zip. Zilch. I'm even trying to get into a university here, which has been put off, for the time being, at least.

I also have a friend here in Germany whose dream is to play in the NBA someday. He's dead set that he's going to make it. He'd been playing ball in the German third league for five or six years and has now made it to the second league. I've been playing basketball in the German third league for eleven years. Trust me, I've been here long enough to know that there is no way that a career-long German third league player is good enough for the NBA, yet this guy won't give up his dream. In one sense, it's admirable, yet in another, it's also depressing. It's good to have dreams, but we also need to be realistic and see when the dream is not going to happen or when it just isn't possible.

Sometimes dreams die. They just do. It may be they never had a beginning, or they might be pipe dreams from the beginning. But with God's confirmation of our dreams, we can take action rather than just sitting around day-dreaming about a better world.

God has confirmed my dreams in a way that was similar to how He confirmed Nehemiah's. He won't allow me to let it go. I can't wake up without thinking of riding my bike with a bunch of guys through mountains. I can't go to bed without thinking of what to write next. God has put these dreams in me and won't let me forget them.

How can I explain basically writing in secret, except for some sarcastic, dry-humored emails to friends and then having a friend who just happens to own a publishing license to ask me if I wanted to write? Is that a coincidence? I think not. As this friend wrote in an email: "There are no coincidences with God."

I was still a little skeptical until I sent my friend some of my writing, and he passed them on to some of his colleagues, who really liked what I wrote. *Other people were actually impacted by something I wrote.* I'm not bragging. I'm simply saying that all along God has been showing me His confirmation for this dream.

And can I explain in any other way, other than confirmation, God providing ways for me to cycle here in Europe? A guy has wanted me to go on a tour with him for the past three years, and it's just now working out. I was finally able to get a nice bike and find a good friend, who is also interested in cycling and touring— open doors. My cycling dream is taking shape.

Dream on, indeed!

XIV.
GOD'S CONFIRMATION OF DREAMS

Is God really the author of our dreams? If we have a dream how can we be sure the idea has really come from God rather than it just being something we desire. This is a legitimate quandary to battle through if we are committed to living in obedience and don't want to waste our time doing something God doesn't want us doing.

Some of you may be wondering if it is even possible to know if those dreams inside you are really from God? I think it is. I ended the last chapter talking about God confirming things in my life concerning my dreams, and I think that you can know what is from God.

Let's go back to Nehemiah, let's look in the New Testament, and then let's come back to today.

I think a great sign of confirmation could be sleeplessness. Ok, I know that doesn't sound too wonderful, a life without sleep. But I've experienced this in two different ways. The first is in sheer excitement. Knowing that God wants to use me. Knowing that I have this dream that is welling up inside me. Longing to live it out. And I can't sleep because I have these ideas. And I'm rehashing old ideas. Mixing them up with new ideas. And all I can do is think about it. Tossing and turning. The dream is growing right in front of my wide-open eyes. I can only think of U2's *Bad*, as Bono is screaming the words, "I'm wiiiide awaaaaake! I'm wiiiide awaaaaake!" and then he sings softly, "I'm not sleeping." That's the fun kind of sleeplessness.

The second comes from heaviness of heart. And this is not fun. You can't sleep because your heart is broken just like Nehemiah, or you can't sleep because you feel heaviness on your chest or a loss of breath.

What could that heaviness be about? What about that loss of breath? I honestly believe this heaviness on our chests, or this loss of breath, could be demons doing their best to torture us. I've talked to other Christian friends who feel the same way, so I don't feel too alone in this. I don't mean to sound spooky or hocus-pocus, nor do I want to try and over-spiritualize everything. But think about it this way, or better yet, ask yourself this question: "Why would a demon want me to feel good about pursuing my dream if it would help impact God's Kingdom in a positive way for eternity?"

Again, if you are on the verge, or in the middle, of doing something for God, do you think demons are sitting around thinking, "Oh look, the little Christian is going ahead with his

plans to further dominate us. That's so cute."
No way! They're going to attack! Wouldn't it
make more sense for the "rulers of the darkness
of this world" (Ephesians 6:12) – also known as
demons – to terrorize you into not pursuing your
dreams before you even begin? What would be
easier for Satan than defeating us in battles that
we haven't even begun fighting?

I've been there. I have experienced peri-
ods of my life when I know there's no uncon-
fessed sin in my life, I'm doing what God wants,
I'm experiencing time of amazing communion
with my Father, yet I can't breathe or sleep. I'm
just tossing and turning in my bed and something, or someone, is making my life miserable.

That leads us to another method of confirmation—resistance. If your dream is from
God and is purposefully honoring God, then
keep your eyes open. In 1 Corinthians 16:13,
Paul says: "Be on the alert, stand firm in the
faith, act like men, be strong." If you are pursuing a God-given dream, be on the alert because

an attack is coming. I've said this before, but it is worth repeating. You are dangerous! Satan does not want to see you or your dream prosper. He does not want to see the Kingdom of God expanding.

As frightening as this may be, and as dangerous as it must seem: if Satan is attacking you, you have a good reason to believe you're doing the right thing.

God uses our friends to confirm our dreams too. It's not always easy to see, and we can be misled because our friends might just agree with us because they are our friends, and they want to see us succeed. Nehemiah had the king as a friend—a friend who was willing to help him. His friend, who just happened to be his master, literally helped pave the way for his dream to come true.

And even though Nehemiah had his enemies (more on that in the next chapter), he also had plenty of manpower. Nehemiah 3 is basically the employee list of all those who helped build Jerusalem's walls. Nehemiah wasn't alone; he had plenty of help from men who believed in his dream too. If you know your dream is touching the lives of others, you might be on to something.

And here's the final confirmation that your dream is from God—God's blessing. Is God letting the dream take place? Is it all "working" out? Is it actually happening? Then maybe, my fellow dreamer, your dream is coming true because God is helping it along the way!

We can always make the argument that all kinds of people have had their dreams come true, whether they were living their lives for God or not. Quite true. Even David lamented about this throughout the Psalms. While his enemies were prospering all around him, he was God's own chosen king and was running around hiding in caves to stay alive. The irony and injustice was not lost on David. It's safe to say that the godless will prosper too. Don't forget this is a spiritual war, and Satan is going to do his best to make sure his pawns are in place too.

If God is truly behind our dreams, won't He, in His almighty power, make sure His cause wins in the end? In Nehemiah 2:8, we read: "God was showing kindness to me," and then in verse 18, "...how God had been kind to me".

God had given Nehemiah his dream, He provided help through the king, He provided help through fellow-workers, He provided the material, He kept all the opposition at bay (see next chapter), and best of all, He was glorified when the dream was fulfilled.

After the walls are built around Jerusalem, the Israelites begin returning. The nation of Israel is back. Not only are they back, but they begin confessing their sins and start the healing process of returning to their God. The walls were just a part of the dream. The whole dream revolved around God's chosen people coming back to Him and becoming what He had created them to be.

I recently came across three passages that illustrate how bad God wants us to come to Him with our dreams. He wants us to ask Him for help, because He wants to be an integral part.

At the end of Psalm 90, Moses writes: "Lord our God, treat us well. *Give us success* in what we do; yes, *give us success* in what we do" (emphasis mine). And in Psalm 118, the psalmist writes: "Please Lord, save us; please Lord, *give us success*" (emphasis mine).

How will you know if your dream is from God? Well, if you go to Him and ask Him for help, and He does help, is that not confirmation enough? Just read what John wrote in 1 John 5:14: "And this is the boldness we have in God's presence ..." Stop right there. Wait a second. We can have boldness in God's presence? We can be bold in God's presence? We don't have to have any fear? Are you starting to see the picture here? God doesn't want a generation of weak Christians. He wants men and women who can be bold. He wants us to be more than we are. He wants us to rise up with wings like eagles!

The verse continues: "And this is the boldness we have in God's presence: that if we ask God for anything that agrees with what he wants, he hears us." If our dreams are in conjunction with what God wants, He's going to hear us. He's proved over and over that He will help. Nehemiah is proof of that. The nation of Israel is proof of that. Martin Luther's dream of a readable Bible for the people is proof of that.

Of course, there's the other type of confirmation as well. The kind that says: "No!" The negative confirmation we just don't want to hear. Maybe age, lack of ability, or timing is keeping us from achieving our dreams. Maybe it is reality settling in, or maybe it's something greater than that. In other words, maybe God is just saying, "No." Maybe it's a "No....for now," or maybe it's a, "No. Period. End of story."

God did not give me the talent for a career in the NBA. Or the talent to play Division 1 basketball, for that matter. My dreams did not fall into what God wanted. "No. Period. End of story." My dream to write never came into fruition until the right friends came into my life. "No...for now...be patient."

Look at David. He was supposed to be the King of Israel and what is he doing during his developmental years? Raising sheep. Sheep! The future king of Israel...raising sheep! Smelly, dumb sheep. Sounds fun, eh? No! Not if you're a dreamer. So what does he do while he's waiting and keeping Fluffy the Sheep from being eaten by bears and lions? Well, besides killing those bears and lions to protect Fluffy the Sheep, he practices flicking his sling around and he practices his harp. What ends up happening? He ends up toppling a giant (and consequently an entire army) with a stone and a sling. And he ends up being the author of songs/psalms that we are still singing and studying today!

Maybe your dream isn't coming to fruition because you are the one calling the shots. I have had things that I've wanted to accomplish, which have not happened. I wanted to run basketball camps all around Germany. I wanted to do it for my family and myself—not for God. Guess what? I'm not running camps right now. God took the joy out of it for me. I was focused on myself and my dream and any financial success I could possibly achieve rather than how I could live for God.

In the Bible, this point is illustrated perfectly in the Isaiah 50:10-11:

> *Who among you fears the Lord and obeys his servant? That person may walk in the dark and have no light. Then let him trust in the Lord and depend on his God. But instead, some of you want to light your own fires and make your own light. So, go, walk in the light of your fires, and trust your own light to guide you. But this is what you will receive from me: You will lie down in a place of pain.*

How many times have I tried to light my own fires? I can't even begin to count. Why didn't I find this verse before? What a warning, straight from God—do it your way and suffer the consequences. What a contrast to being able to come to God in boldness and have Him bless you?

James is also very clear about the consequences of living our lives just for us. He records in chapter 4:

> *You want things, but you do not have them. So you are ready to kill and are jealous of other people, but you still cannot get what you want. So you argue and fight. You do not get what you want, because you do not ask God. Or when you ask, you do not receive because the reason you ask is wrong. You want things so you can use them for your own pleasures.*

You want the truth? I hate that passage. Sometimes the Bible is so convicting. Okay, I don't hate that passage, but I hate reading that passage. Why? Because it tells me exactly how I have been living my life. I've been living my life for me. I've been jealous and angry. Maybe not ready to kill, but certainly not in the best of moods.

Sometimes God is very clear about His confirmation of our dreams, and we need to be ready to hear the answer. When God says, "Yes," we need to get up and go. We need to move. Now. But if God says "No," we need to ponder why.

XV.
THE CHALLENGE
AGAINST THE DREAM

How do dreams die? In many cases, I think it is reality. I dreamt of playing in the NBA. A few things kept me from playing basketball at the highest level. First of all, I'm too slow. I'm also not as talented as the other players, and I'm not a great shooter, dribbler, or rebounder—in other words, I don't have a great command of the skills I need for basketball that would allow me to play at that level. To put it plainly: I'm simply not good enough. To continue to dream and plan for something that is not going to happen would be foolish.

What about the dreams that are still in your heart that reality hasn't closed the doors on yet? How do those dreams die? Personally, I think those dreams are stolen or murdered by the Devil himself.

Do you think Satan wants to see you become all that you can be? If you're a Christian trying to live for God, do you think the Devil is going to sit back and watch you thrive? If you do, you've got another thing coming! Rest assured, once you begin to take your God-given dreams seriously, Satan will attack. Satan will attack you. There is no way that the Devil is going to let his enemy run roughshod all over him.

I knew a man who was a promising baseball player as young man (you can cue Bruce

Springsteen's *Glory Days* now, if you want). He was really good. He was getting minor league offers out of high school. The guy was a stud pitcher. Another kid I knew from my own high school was a promising hockey player—a bit undersized but an incredible player. He was getting letters from colleges as a sophomore! We're talking about, in one case, someone potentially becoming a big league pitcher and, in another case, if not making it professionally, having a free college education through a hockey scholarship. You know what happened? Neither one of them made it. You want to know why? Drugs. Both guys ended up drinking and smoking their way out of future success. The Devil is a murderer, according to Christ (John 8:44), and if he can't get us, he might as well kill what we could be.

Remember, Satan is clever. He doesn't always need to kill our dreams himself. Introducing drugs or something extreme into our lives doesn't have to be his only modus operandi. Why do the work if someone else will? Someone like you or me, for example.

I believe Satan uses us to kill our own dreams. He whispers in our ears and plants seeds of doubt in us: "That's impossible," "There is no way you can get enough people to work with you on that," "You're too old," "You're too young," or "You're not skilled enough for that."

Look back at Nehemiah and what he had to overcome. Getting a paid vacation was not exactly the kind of thing a slave requests of the king. Asking for safe travel and for building materials were not exactly the kinds of things a slave would ask the king. I can think of some grounds for doubt here. Just think what would have happened if Nehemiah had listened to the doubts in his head.

I met a guy once who became a team-mate of mine in a local men's basketball league. This guy was a really good player. He could do everything: shoot three's, play near the basket, and use his body for what we call "body advantages." He understood how to have people move on the court so his team could score, and he was a hard worker and a really good passer. He's the kind of guy every coach would love to have on his team. Plus, he watched every game possible on TV. He studied the game, so he could get learn as much as possible. But there was a problem.

This guy was playing in men's leagues almost every night trying to recapture a dream. He was one of the best players I've ever played with, but he never played college ball. He never got the chance to play college basketball because he never played in high school. And you know why he didn't play in high school? Because he "was scared to go out for the team." Those are his words. He was scared of the potential rejection of being cut from the team. And the worst part? You know who told him he wasn't good enough? He did! He listened to the doubts in his head which said, "You're not good enough. You'll never make the team."

He is a perfect example of what listening to our doubts and never letting a dream grow looks like. The Devil whispers what he wants us to believe, and we do the rest.

There's yet another way the Devil will kill our dreams—through words of criticism from others. They can come from friends, from foes, very often, and most painfully, from family. John Eldredge relates a story of a father's stinging words to his son in *Wild at Heart*.

"I don't remember all that was said, but I do remember his last words: 'You are such a mama's boy,' he yelled at me. Then he walked out." ... And so those words fell like a final blow, a *death sentence*. (emphasis mine)

Let's face it, words hurt. They wound us in ways that no physical blow can. Words from family are the most painful, but there's no way you can deny that words from foes or peers don't hurt.

When I was a freshman in high school, I was 5'0" and 97 lbs. I was in no way, shape, or form an intimidating physical specimen. There was no way I should have been anywhere near a basketball team—other than being the water boy. But I had dreams. I dreamed of being on my high school team. I wanted to make my dad proud, so I busted my butt to be ready for the tryouts.

There were two kids in my class, Brad and Mike, who felt it was their personal responsibility to make my life a living hell in high school. The physical abuse stopped after a while (probably because I pinned Mike to the ground in gym class—never a good thing for a bully when the smallest kid in a hundred-mile radius is on top of him). The verbal abuse continued: "You'll never make the team," "You suck," and "Why are you even trying?" "Even if you do make the team, you'll never play." Ah, the wonderful world of peer pressure. I grew a very real and honest disdain for those guys.

I originally went out for basketball to please my father (the fact that he promised me a car if I made the team may also have played a small role in this). But it was the words of Mike and Brad that lit a fire in me that is still going today. I made the team, I ended up eventually starting, eventually made varsity, eventually became All-Conference and All-Area, eventually played small college ball, and eventually played pro ball in Germany.

Guess whom I couldn't wait to see at my ten-year class reunion? And guess who wasn't there? The fact that they weren't there didn't completely ruin my night, but honestly I was looking forward to seeing those guys. Blast it all!

We need to go back to Nehemiah to further emphasize the point of having your dreams challenged by criticism. The criticism he was getting was a lot worse than two pimple-faced, high school punks telling him that he "sucked."

Nehemiah is pretty wound about being on the job. He can't even sleep. In the second chapter, we see that he goes out at night to inspect everything. His adrenaline must have been running through him like a torrent. He was probably thinking about what guys could be working on the west side, who was best fit for the heavy lifting, who would be best fit for leadership. He was probably making to-do lists and figuring out the meal schedule for all of the workers. He was probably as excited as he could be.

His dream was coming true. God had provided everything he needed and given him the green light at every intersection. And now, he was at the job site and ready to go.

But the verbal barbs were soon to come:

> But when Sanballat the Horonite, Tobiah the Ammonite officer, and Geshem the Arab heard about it, they made fun of us and laughed at us. They said, "What are you doing? Are you turning against the king?"
> But I answered them, "The God of heaven will give us success…" (Nehemiah 2:19, 20a)

Focus! Sure he was getting made fun of, but Nehemiah kept his eyes on his dream and on God, Who was helping the dream come true.

The beginning of chapter four shows Sanballat and Tobiah again making fun of the Israelites. But this time they are "angry" and "furious" (v. 1). What does Nehemiah do? He prays. He stays focused on the source of his dream. He turns to God.

One could argue that Nehemiah was just being thick-skinned. That we—when we face adversity—shouldn't let people's words get us down. Let the words roll of our backs. Nehemiah is a good example here, but maybe it's a lesson we've already known before, right? The old, "sticks and stones" argument.

Well, I beg to differ. Starting in verse 7, we see just how well Nehemiah knows his detractors. He knows these are some seriously bad dudes. These men had "made plans to come to Jerusalem and fight and stir up trouble" (v. 8).

And it gets even worse! In chapter 6, we read that Nehemiah is being lured, by these same men, out into the desert for a meeting. A meeting of the minds, it was not—think *Sopranos* or *The God Father*. Think whack-job. These guys wanted Nehemiah dead. They were so angry and furious with this guy that they wanted to murder him!

They wanted to kill him. They wanted him dead.

That is some pretty serious resistance to his dream, but Nehemiah never gave up. He did two things every single time his dream was threatened. He went straight to God, and he kept working towards his dream.

It doesn't matter how Satan kills our dreams—through nasty words, seeds of doubts, threats, the lure of something else. It just doesn't matter. If you stop working towards your dream, it will never happen. Period.

What would have happened if Dr. King had never started organizing marches in the South? What if he had listened to the people who told him he was a second-class citizen, or given in to the death threats he received? What would have happened if Einstein had listened to his teachers? What would have happened if Sally Ride hadn't dreamed of being an astronaut? What would have happened if Martin Luther had given up on his dream to translate the entire New Testament into the language of the people because the job would have taken too long? What would have happened if he had cowered before the Pope's death sentence?

What's going to happen to your dream if you keep sleeping on it?

XVI.
CARPE DEIM II

So, now what do we do? Great question. Somewhere in the middle of this book I asked the question, "Where do we go now?" Just where do we go, and what do we do once we get there?

Well, I think it's pretty simple really. Honestly. Sometimes everything in life gets so confusing and it seems like we can't see out of the fog that we're in. Other times it seems that we are making things more complicated than we need to—we are the ones fogging our lives up. I know that's the case in my own life. I end up taking matters into my own hands and making everything worse when the simplicity in everything lies in Christ.

God tells us that we are His children, not Satan's. God tells us that we are pure, not full of sin. God tells us that we were made to be something wonderful, not slugs who need to fight through this life.

Where do we go? We run to God! We run from Satan. And then in the embraces of our Father, we turn and look Satan in the face realizing something more than magical. We realize Satan is ours to rule over. He has no say whatsoever in our lives!

This discovery has freed my conscience. I'm no longer burdened with guilt over sins in my past. I'm more concerned with the sins of "now" and trying to defeat those through God's power, but I'm not the miserable, defeated sinner I once was. I rule over sin! This discovery also means that the battle has just begun. Again, once Satan has lost us—and we know it and we live like it—he's coming after us with all the fury of hell.

But once we are there, in God's arms, we wake up. We wake up from the slumber that we were in, and we see the truth of our lives and what we were made to be. But we also wake up to dream!

Paul quoted from numerous passages from Isaiah when he wrote to the Ephesians; "Wake up, sleeper, rise from death, and Christ will shine on you" (Eph. 5:14)

Wake up! Wake up out of our death, and Christ will shine on us. He will light us up and make us *alive*. And going back to John 10:10, Christ promises to give us a life that is abundant and overflowing. In other words, our lives will be alive!

And now that we are alive, does it make sense to live like we're dead? Why would we want to live like a dead person? A great illustration is from the movie The *Shawshank Redemption*. It's the story of Andy Dufresne, a young man sent to prison, and taken under the tutelage of an old inmate, Red. Living in prison is not exactly the greatest of occupations, and yet, even in prison, Andy never gives up hope. He comes up with this credo:

"Get busy living, or get busy dying."

And guess what? We're not in prison! At least not in a spiritual prison, held captive by Satan. No, we're free. We are free in Christ! And we are alive. It's time to "get busy living!"

I'm not the biggest rap music fan. Nor am I the world's biggest Eminem fan (he does make me laugh sometimes, although I will deny it under oath). But his song *Lose Yourself*, from the *8 Mile* soundtrack, is a great song about grabbing the moment and seizing

your dream. He is basically confronting the pos-
sibility in his life that he may only have one
chance to accomplish his dream and he's going
to go for it. If he's going to fail, it's not because
he didn't try. Here is an excerpt from Lose
Yourself (ignore the grammatical errors, he's
from Detroit—and since I'm from Chicago, I'm
entitled to at least one Detroit insult per book):

*Look, if you had one shot, one opportunity/To
seize everything you every wanted…One
moment/Would you capture it or just let it slip?*

*His palms are sweaty, knees weak, arms are
heavy…/He's nervous, but on the surface he
looks calm and ready…/He choked…/He's so
mad, but he won't give up that/Is he? No/He
won't have it…/Back to the lab again…*

*You better lose yourself in the music, the
moment/You own it, you better never let it
go/You only get one shot, do not miss your
chance to blow/This opportunity comes once in
a lifetime yo*

The soul's escaping, through this hole that it's gaping/This world is mine for the taking...

Mom, I love you, but this trail has got to go/I cannot grow old in Salem's lot
So here I go is my shot/Feet fail me not cuz maybe the only opportunity that I got

Here he is with a dream. His dream was to be a rapper and to get out from where he was—living in a trailer park in Detroit. He wanted out. He wanted to be alive. His only way out (or so he thought) was through rap music, and he wouldn't let the dream die or run from the opportunities to make the dream happen.

This song (if you choose to call a rap a song) is an inspiration to go for it. And yet this song has nothing to do with God or living for God. How much more inspirational is it to realize that your dream could be used by God! And that your dream could have ramifications that last throughout eternity!

Let's end with the conclusion. Not the book's conclusion, but our lives' conclusions. Death. Six feet under. No more breath coming from our lungs.

I don't fear death. Death is mine, remember? Yes, it will eventually take me, but where is it taking me? That's right! Death is just my vehicle to heaven. But I must confess, I do fear death right now. And I do not want Christ to return right now.

Christ is returning, that we are promised. I am either going to be gathered together with his children upon His return or I will die and be in His presence. Either way, I'm going to be in God's Kingdom. That I am confident of.

But I just woke up. The day is young, and there is so much to do. And I am just now realizing that God has given me a dream, and He's paving the way for this dream to happen. I have to tell you I want to live this dream out! I want to make it happen.

But not for me. It's not about me doing my thing. Although it may sound like that, that is not why I want to accomplish my dreams. We can look all around us and see people living out their dreams, making money, going on vacations, buying new things, climbing up the corporate ladder, gaining power, playing in bands, playing in sports, etc. And all of those people, including me, dream of success. I think that's normal. I'm not sure anyone says, "I want to be the worst _____, ever!" or "I want to have the worst career possible." We want to succeed, that's normal. God wants us to succeed.

But to what end? What's the point of achieving all my goals at the expense of my family? What's the point of accumulating money or things, when, as the old adage says: "you can't take it with you"? I want to let you in on a little secret. "You can't take it with you" is only half true. You do take something with you. The question is: what will you take with you?

You don't take things with you. I can't take my basketball shoes, my laptop, or my U2 CD collection, and I certainly can't take my Porsche 911 (ok, I don't really have one, but if I did, I still couldn't take it with me). But Paul tells us in 1 Corinthians 3 that we will take something with us.

We take our works. We take what we did with our lives with us. Paul is not saying that we can work our way to Heaven. The Bible is very clear that Christ is the only way to the Kingdom of God. Paul is saying that once we are under God's grace, through Christ's blood, we have a life to live and at the end of the day, there will be a judgment. A Holy Judgment. And God is going to put our works on an altar. And He's going to light our works on fire. And burn them. God is going to take what we have done with our lives, and judge them, to see if what we did was worthy of His Kingdom, or not.

And all the things that we did with our lives that were for us, for our own gain are going to be consumed in that fire. They will be rendered useless. Nothing. My wealth (all $42.67) will be nothing. My great music collection will be melted away. Those cool clothes that I have—gone. My bike! My precious bike with all the newest technology and carbon forks will be just a memory.

I'm scared. I'm scared my life is going to have nothing to offer God. That's why I don't want Him to come back yet. I want to be able to give Him something. I don't want to go to God's Kingdom empty-handed.

I want God to look at my life and burn all the junk away, and I want to be able to show Him that I touched millions of people's lives through books. That I showed young men Christ through riding a bike up and down mountains. I want God to say something like, "Well done.

You had dreams. You lived your life for me, and you taught others to wake up and dream and the entire world woke up and saw Me, and came to Me. Well done."

That's why Paul told the Christians living in Rome to offer their lives a living sacrifice. That's why God allowed Paul's writings to survive. So generations of Christians, over thousands of years, would be encouraged to sacrifice their lives a living sacrifice. Again, living life!

How do you want to go to God? Ask yourself what is it that is burning inside of you? If you could do something in this world that could change the future of the world for Christ's sake, what would it be? If you could live, really live, really feel alive—wouldn't you grab that opportunity?

RISE UP

Wouldn't you seize the day?

For God's Kingdom...*Carpe Diem*!

WANT MORE FROM
CONSUMED MINISTRIES?

Check us out on the web!

www.consumedministries.com

Where you can learn more about Consumed,
and find other books by Consumed Publishing.

Or...

Listen to our podcast...

We can be found on itunes!

Or...

Tune in to our radio broadcasts!
(in select US cities)